Puppy Miracles

True, Inspirational Stories of
Our Lovable, Furry Friends

Brad Steiger and Sherry Hansen Steiger

ADAMS MEDIA
Avon, Massachusetts

Published by
Adams Media, an F+W Publications Company
57 Littlefield Street, Avon, MA 02322. U.S.A.
www.adamsmedia.com

ISBN 10: 1-59337-535-2
ISBN 13: 978-1-59337-535-5

Printed in the United States of America.

J I H G F E D C

Library of Congress Cataloging-in-Publication Data
Steiger, Brad.
Puppy miracles / by Brad Steiger and Sherry Hansen Steiger.
p.   cm.
ISBN-13: 978-1-59337-535-5
ISBN-10: 1-59337-535-2
1. Puppies--Anecdotes. 2. Dog owners--Anecdotes. 3. Human-animal rela-
tionships--Anecdotes. I. Steiger, Sherry Hansen. II. Title.
SF426.2.S674 2006
636.7'07--dc22
2006019731

This publication is designed to provide accurate and authoritative information with regard to the subject matter covered. It is sold with the understanding that the publisher is not engaged in rendering legal, accounting, or other professional advice. If legal advice or other expert assistance is required, the services of a competent professional person should be sought.

—From a *Declaration of Principles* jointly adopted by a Committee of the American Bar Association and a Committee of Publishers and Associations

Many of the designations used by manufacturers and sellers to distinguish their products are claimed as trademarks. Where those designations appear in this book and Adams Media was aware of a trademark claim, the designations have been printed with initial capital letters.

While all the events and experiences recounted in this book are true and happened to real people, some of the names, dates, and places have been changed in order to protect the privacy of certain individuals.

Photograph ©Herbert Spichtinger/Zefa/Corbis.

This book is available at quantity discounts for bulk purchases.
For information, call 1-800-289-0963.

Puppy Miracles

TRUE, INSPIRATIONAL STORIES OF OUR LOVABLE, FURRY FRIENDS

Foreword

Good Advice from a Very Perceptive Puppy (Anonymous)

When loved ones come home, always run to greet them.
Take naps.
Stretch before rising.
Run, romp, and play daily.
Never pass up the opportunity to go for a joyride.
Allow the experience of fresh air and the wind in your
    face to be pure ecstasy.
When it's in your best interest, always practice obedience.
Let others know when they've invaded your territory.
Thrive on attention and let people touch you.
Avoid biting when a simple growl will do.
On warm days, stop to lie on your back in the grass.
On hot days, drink lots of water and lie under a shady
    tree.
When you're happy, dance around and wag your
    entire body.
No matter how often you're scolded, don't buy into the
    guilt thing and pout. Run right back and make
    friends.

Delight in the simple joy of a long walk.

Eat with gusto and enthusiasm. Stop when you've had enough.

Be loyal.

Never pretend to be something you're not.

If you want what lies buried, dig until you find it.

When someone is having a bad day, be silent, sit close by, and nuzzle him or her gently.

*C*harles M. Schulz, the creator of the classic comic strip *Peanuts*, summarized the human-dog relationship so well when he said, "Happiness is a warm puppy." The hundreds of men and women who over the years have shared with us their stories of a lifelong love of dogs agree: People never forget the excitement and the joy that they experienced as children when they got their first puppy. The wonderful relationship between a child and a puppy was also the beginning of learning important lessons about taking care of another being, and about recognizing the place of all creatures—great and small—in the web of life.

There are more than 60 million Americans who share their households with dogs. What better time to write a book about puppies, than the year traditional Chinese astrology designates as the Year of the Dog?

Dog owners or not, few people can resist the fuzzy face of a puppy or the desire to pick it up and hold it. Decades ago, savvy advertisers learned that the ads and commercials drawing the most positive and productive attention were not those depicting their products paired with a lovely lady in a swimsuit, but the ones coupling their wares with a happy child and an affectionate puppy.

Puppy Miracles is filled with heartwarming stories of inspiration, courage, and devotion, demonstrating the remarkable depth of feeling that exists between humans and canines. It also explores the bond of unconditional love that provides so many individuals with life-altering experiences. Within these pages, you will be able to experience the truth that happiness, harmony, health, and healing can be found in the warmth and love of a puppy.

Brad Steiger
Sherry Hansen Steiger
November 2006

Puppy Miracles

Puppy Miracles

TRUE, INSPIRATIONAL STORIES OF OUR LOVABLE, FURRY FRIENDS

*D*ogs are often hailed as "angels without wings," especially when they are involved in rescuing humans from dangerous situations. Although we sincerely hope such terrible circumstances as those that befell Mrs. Dragica Vlaco would never happen to you, just try to imagine what it would be to fall into a river at night, to crawl shivering and cold up on the bank, to feel that your life is nearly over—and then to look up and see a dog, complete with halo and wings, standing over you.

On October 29, 2002, Buoy, a yellow Labrador retriever, and his owner Jim Simpson were attending a Halloween party on Gowen Avenue, near the Columbia River, in Richland, Washington. Because it was a costume party, Simpson had outfitted Buoy, who was known for his pleasant disposition and friendliness toward people, as an angel, with a halo around his head and wings attached to his body.

Around 8:30 P.M., Buoy indicated that he needed to take a break to obey nature's call and Simpson let him outside. After a few minutes, Simpson called for the Labrador to return to the party. Concerned that the usually promptly obedient dog did not heed his calls, Simpson decided that he should investigate and see what had delayed or halted Buoy's return.

After walking a bit along the footpath near the levee, Simpson told the Richland *Tri-City Herald* that he sighted Buoy at the bottom of a rocky slope that jutted into the river. The Labrador answered his owner's summons with several anxious barks of his own, and it was clear that Buoy had discovered something near the water that he believed superseded Simpson's calls to return to the party. When Simpson investigated, he was shocked to find that Buoy's concerns centered around a woman who was lying on the ground, disoriented, soaking wet, and shivering uncontrollably in the 20°F temperatures. Buoy was nudging and licking the woman, trying his best to help her. Simpson could clearly see that Buoy had resolved to remain rooted to the spot until help came.

Simpson immediately summoned the police and an ambulance. Later, Simpson learned that the woman's name was Dragica Vlaco, and that her family had been searching for her since that afternoon. Police theorized that Mrs. Vlaco had become disoriented from the pain medications that she had been taking for a recent shoulder surgery, wandered down to the levee, and fell into the river. She was taken to the Kadlec Medical Center, treated for hypothermia, and released a few days later.

There was no question in anyone's mind that Buoy had found Mrs. Vlaco just in time. She would surely have frozen to death if she had lain unprotected and unnoticed for very much longer.

Simpson commented to a reporter, "Buoy's a pretty friendly dog and pretty curious about people. It's a good thing he went over there and found the woman when he did."

And appearing garbed as an angel probably contributed a great deal to Mrs. Vlaco's state of mind.

*I*f you should ever find yourself alone in subzero temperatures, Charlie Brown's observation that, "happiness is a warm puppy," would take on a whole new meaning. When Desmond Pemberton, fifty-eight, lay unable to move in the cold Kaimanawa Forest Park on the North Island of New Zealand, he had only his puppy, B, to keep him from freezing to death. Thankfully, B was enough.

Pemberton, wearing only a pair of polar fleece pants, a polypropylene singlet, a T-shirt, and a bush shirt, set out on Wednesday, August 8, 2001, in his Suzuki four-wheel drive SUV accompanied by B, his Labrador–blue heeler mix, for a brief outing in the park. Pemberton, who was in remission from lung cancer and also suffered from emphysema, perhaps overexerted himself on the drive and collapsed at the steering wheel, sending the Suzuki and its passengers crashing into a ravine.

For five days and nights, Pemberton fell in and out of consciousness. Temperatures fell to four degrees below zero, and for three nights, icy rain fell. The only thing that kept Pemberton from freezing was B, his faithful companion, who snuggled up against Pemberton to keep him warm.

On Monday, August 13, a forest survey helicopter spotted the crashed Suzuki SUV near Sika Lodge, about thirty-six miles southeast of Taupo. Upon investigating, they found the nearly dead Pemberton. At his side, in the wreckage in the ravine, was Pemberton's faithful B.

The *New Zealand Herald* reported that Pemberton was frozen and unable to speak when his rescuers located him. One of the men told reporters that Pemberton was so cold that he was, "actually stiff and couldn't even open his mouth." Senior Constable Barry Shepherd added that the man was suffering from hypothermia and would almost certainly have died if he had suffered such exposure to the cold for one more night. Medical experts said that Pemberton had been kept alive by the warmth of his dog, who slept by his side when temperatures plunged.

At any time, B could have struck out on his own and probably would have reached shelter and food within two or three days. However, B chose to remain by his owner's side and place his master's survival above his own.

*L*ee Moorhead of Long Island, New York, told us that she had a wonderful story for us regarding a puppy miracle:

"When my daughter Gigi was only ten days old, I gave my husband a German shepherd puppy for Father's Day, because I learned that he had wanted one all his life. We named her Princess, and she took to our family immediately and was very protective of our little girl.

"When my son Michael, now a grown man, was born, Princess guarded his crib as if she were with the FBI. No one, not even my in-laws, could approach the crib without her barking up a storm to let me know someone was in the room. When Mike was big enough to prop up in a highchair, he would sit there and feed Princess his baby cookies. She would take a bite, and then he would take a bite, until the cookie was all gone.

"Before Michael was born, I worked in New York City for an advertising firm. Although I was on an extended maternity leave, my boss called one day and begged me to come to the office long enough to break in a new secretary. Michael was still crawling and just a baby, but I complied and did my best to show the new lady the special talents and abilities needed for working at an advertising firm. After six months or so, the firm called and said that the lady I had trained so diligently did not work out, and they asked me back again to break in another new secretary. I hired a housekeeper, Mrs. Dumphy, to take care of my three-year-old daughter and my baby son.

"One day when I got home from work, my housekeeper was very distraught. Mrs. Dumphy told me that if it were not for Princess, I might have lost my son that day. We lived up a very high flight of stairs on the second floor of a two-family house, and the hallway was a tiled floor. Mrs. Dumphy never noticed that the door to the apartment was open slightly. Somehow, Michael escaped through the door and made his way to the top step. Princess jumped in front of him and started barking loudly. Mrs. Dumphy did not hear Princess's alarm at first because she was doing dishes and the water was running, drowning out the dog's bark. When she turned off the water, she could hear Princess barking and ran out to find her blocking Michael with her body. He would certainly have fallen down that long flight of steps and landed on the tile in the hallway.

"Princess was a very special dog, and our family loved her dearly. Unfortunately, she died when having puppies just a few years later. We took her out to my husband's parents' house in the country to bury her under an oak tree. I wrote a letter to Mike that day about how Princess had saved his life. I gave him the letter when he turned twenty-one."

*A*ll dog owners will remember the first time their "fearless" four-legged fur ball heard thunder. The puppy's eyes opened wider than you'd ever seen them; an anxious whine came from deep inside the wee body; all four paws began tap-dancing nervously on the floor; and, if at all possible, the normally brave and bold pup crawled up on your lap for safety.

Some dogs, albeit a very small percentage, don't seem to pay much attention to thunder, let alone exhibit unrestrained fear and trembling. However, most canines do respond, according to the definition of thunder in the *The Dog's Dictionary*, which explains the atmospheric phenomenon as "…a signal that the world is coming to an end. Humans remain amazingly calm during thunderstorms, so it is necessary to warn them of the danger by trembling uncontrollably, panting, rolling your eyes wildly, and following at their heels." For all those insensitive humans who laugh and make light of such canine concerns about thunder, there is the story of Sport to stop the cynics cold in their tracks. Sport nearly paid the ultimate price for learning that when thunder rumbles across the heavens, everyone should be afraid—*very afraid*.

On Wednesday, April 24, 2002, Sally Andis, who lived in rural Washington, Indiana, stepped inside just as a thunderstorm was beginning to pelt down rain. Sport, her little beagle, was just outside the backdoor, chained to a nearby tree.

There was the sound of thunder and the flash of lightning. Sally heard Sport let out a yelp—then she couldn't see anything. All the lights in the house went out. Every appliance in the house had its cord blown away from the electrical outlets.

Sally had been standing near the backdoor when a bolt of lightning struck nearby, and the loud sound had deafened her right ear. She stumbled about for a few moments, disoriented. Later, she would remember that everything looked as if it were in some kind of strange fog.

After a few more moments of confusion, Sally's mind cleared and she became filled with concern for her little beagle, chained to the tree where the lightning bolt had struck. She became desperate with fear when she saw that the heat of the lightning strike had left a charred ring around the tree and melted through Sport's chain. Bits of the chain were scattered on the ground, but there was no beagle in sight.

Thinking she heard sounds coming from the nearby creek, Sally ran to investigate and found her little Sport trying to soak up as much water as possible. His fur was singed, and he was bleeding from one paw. When she picked him up, his body felt hot and he was panting. After a while, Sport seemed to regain his equilibrium, and after a detailed examination, the veterinarian proclaimed him unharmed. The singed hair would grow back, and the beagle would be none the worse for having undergone such an *enlightening* experience.

The *Washington Times-Herald* carried a story of the miracle beagle who survived being struck by lightning. It was apparent that the lightning bolt had hit the tree in the Andises' backyard, traveled through Sport's chain, melted the links that bound him to the tree, then continued its jolting pathway *through the dog* and into the foundation of the house, blasting bricks thirty to forty feet away.

Although the electrified beagle seemed sound of body, Sally Andis told reporters that he now preferred staying *in* the house, rather than romping outdoors in the backyard when storms were brewing.

*W*hen Lee Bellinger, owner of a publishing company in Annapolis, Maryland, was visiting his mother in Charlotte, North Carolina, he made the acquaintance of Bundy, a black Labrador–pit bull mix, that belonged to one of his mother's neighbors. The family had acquired Bundy when he was a cute little puppy, but now that he was nine months old and had become gaunt and sickly due to a bad case of worms, the family decided that it would be too costly for them to nurse him back to health. Bundy was about to be taken to a veterinarian to be put down when Lee decided to give him another chance at life.

Lee spent hundreds of dollars in veterinary bills getting Bundy back in shape. But it turned out that he had made an excellent investment.

In January of 1994, Lee woke up one night to find his room filled with black smoke. Frightened and confused, he tried to find his way to safety. Lee began to choke on the heavy smoke. It was as if he were blind, unable to see a thing—unable to find his way through his own home. He was dizzy and disoriented. Lee dropped to the floor and began to crawl. He had to find a way out fast—or he would soon be dead.

Then he felt Bundy brush up against him. Lee reached up, put a finger in his collar, and said, "Let's go for a walk!"

Confidently taking the lead, the big, black dog brought his owner to the front door and to safety.

Within seconds, Lee's bedroom was engulfed in 600-degree flames. The two-story house sustained $125,000 in damages from the electrical fire. Most important, however, both man and dog escaped serious injury.

Bundy had repaid the debt. He had given his benefactor, Lee Bellinger, *his* second chance at life too.

*I*t is always terrible news whenever one hears about missing children. Other parents who hear the news immediately empathize with the missing children's parents. "What would I be feeling right now if those were my kids out there lost, frightened, cold, and hungry?" Even though the "deep, dark woods" have become archetypal in our contemporary consciousness as a frightening place where children may get lost just as they did in the forests of old, each year kids *do* go missing in the forested areas of the United States. Thankfully, after desperate searches by the family and very often hundreds of volunteers, many are found safe and sound—and very often, dogs are responsible for finding the children before it's too late.

One miserable, late winter's day in 1993, the three Eklund brothers went missing for eighteen hours in the swampy woodlands near Dartmouth, Massachusetts. The oldest, Bryan, was only thirteen; the youngest, Matthew, nine; and Robert Jr. in the middle at eleven.

The boys' father, Robert, told those who had joined him to search for the boys that the three brothers, their dog, Abby, and their friend, twelve-year-old David Choquette, had been out exploring the frozen marshlands. After David and Abby, who were in the lead, crossed a pond, the ice cracked behind them, preventing the Eklund brothers from following them.

Not to worry, the boys had told David. They would get home another way. They were certain that they knew of a shortcut.

David said that he felt capable of finding his way home, so he and Abby, a ten-month-old Labrador–German shepherd mix, set off on the path on the other side of the pond.

David and Abby made it home easily. Bryan, Robert, and Matthew did not.

That night, thirty-five volunteers with flashlights searched the dark, swampy woodlands in heavy rain. They were acutely aware that the young boys had no blankets or camping gear with them. They probably didn't even have a match to light a fire. They would be chilled to the bone. To add to their problems, the rain turned to snow and made the soft ground even more treacherous.

At home, Donna Eklund prayed for the safety of her sons. They needed a miracle.

Abby probably sent up a doggy prayer of her own, and she undoubtedly became concerned that her young owners had not found their way home.

By morning, the search party had grown from thirty-five to 400 people, and every single one of the volunteers and law enforcement officials had the same uncomfortable question repeating itself over and over inside their minds, while they desperately searched for the Eklund brothers: *How long could the boys last in the chilling cold and the heavy rain?*

When she could not stand to wait or to pace nervously one minute longer, Abby slipped unnoticed out of the Eklund house and went in search of the three boys. Using her standard, built-in, dog-detection abilities, Abby found Bryan, Robert, and Matthew quite easily.

Just the sight of Abby raised the boys' spirits. They huddled around her to pool their body heat, and they were encouraged by her presence. If she had been able to find them, so should the search party to be able to.

Abby stayed with the boys until they were found— eighteen hours after they had been reported missing.

Donna Eklund had received her miracle, and her sons were in relatively good condition considering the ordeal that they had been through in the freezing rain, snow, and cold.

As for Abby, well, she was rewarded with a big steak.

*C*oncerned about her infant daughter's overall health, Joan Burns of Sioux Falls, South Dakota, had her doctor carefully examine baby Tiffany. Although nothing was discovered that indicated any serious abnormality or medical condition, the family German shepherd, Peter, seemed ill at ease and insisted on sleeping under Tiffany's crib.

Peter proved to be such an attentive caretaker that he saved tiny Tiffany Burns's life twice—in the span of nine months. The infant was only nine days old when the German shepherd pup came running into her mother's bedroom and persuaded her to follow him back to the child's crib.

Joan was horrified to find her baby blue in the face and lying alarmingly still. Thanks to Peter, she got to the crib in time to perform CPR on her infant daughter and to save her life.

Such a demand for immediate attention arose again one night about nine months after the first incident. As he had done before, Peter urgently bounded into the master bedroom to awaken the sleeping mother.

Joan gave Tiffany a cursory once-over and decided that everything was fine.

But when she tried to return to bed, Peter blocked her path. It was unlike the German shepherd to be so aggressive and demanding.

The puzzled mother spent more time, carefully examining her daughter. Nothing. Tiffany was fine.

But Peter, in doggy body language, said *no way*. Joan pushed past him, wanting very much to return to bed and sleep.

Peter followed Joan to her bed and kept at her until she got up once again, this time quite irritated, to go into Tiffany's bedroom to conduct a third examination of the sleeping infant.

It was during her third time checking Tiffany that Joan was horrified to discover that her baby had stopped breathing—just like the time before. She performed CPR with Pete assisting her by licking Tiffany's face.

Later, the doctors theorized that Peter's licking helped stimulate little Tiffany to breathe again. After the doctors completed their examination of Tiffany, their diagnosis discovered symptoms of a rare infant sleeping disorder.

Since the narrow escape of the second episode, Tiffany sleeps with a special monitor that emits a beeping sound should she stop breathing.

Peter, however, isn't taking any chances. He still sleeps under Tiffany's crib.

*C*an you even imagine a person who doesn't like puppies? From the moment of birth, we believe that at least 98 percent of the human species is predisposed to love puppies, and the love affair continues in most folks until they become old and gray. Bring a puppy into a hospital, and the patients' faces light up with smiles. Bring a puppy into a nursing home, and the elderly men and women reach out to touch its fur and receive a flood of memories of times past when they loved a pup of their own.

An astonishing fact about our puppy love is that it is actually good for us. More and more scientists are conducting studies that prove petting a puppy can help humans to lower high blood pressure, to cope with depression, to relieve stress-related disorders, to help children overcome allergies, and to ease the loneliness of the elderly in nursing homes.

Apart from those big, brown puppy eyes looking at us adoringly, apart from giving us an endless supply of unconditional love, apart from our puppies' single-minded mission to please us, why does petting and playing with puppies make us feel so good?

Dr. Karen Allen, associate professor in the School of Medicine at the State University of New York at Buffalo, has found that dogs can help women control stress far more effectively than confiding in a best friend.

In a series of revealing tests, forty-five women had their blood pressure, pulse, skin response, and other bodily functions monitored while they worked on a number of brain-teasing arithmetic problems designed to produce stress and tension. Some of the women tackled the problems with just their dog with them in the testing room. Others performed the tasks in the company of human friends. Interestingly, body responses remained normal among those women who worked with only their dogs present. However, women who had human friends present showed dramatically increased physiological response. Even the presence of very close, supportive human friends caused increased blood pressure, pulse rate, and sweating palms in these stressful problem-solving situations.

Why was this so? Dr. Allen pointed out that we know very well that our dogs don't judge us or evaluate us, and they certainly couldn't care less how we might do on an arithmetic test. The very presence of these human friends made the subjects more likely to rush through the problems and to make mistakes. Dr. Allen said the results clearly demonstrated that the ease with which the tasks were accomplished was much more pronounced with a dog present.

Dr. Allen acknowledged that it is still important to be able to turn to a good friend for support, comfort, and advice, but she admitted that there were many special situations where she would rather be with her dog than a human companion.

As Dr. Alan Beck of the Center for the Human-Animal Bond reminds us, owning a pet isn't just some kind of hobby. Having that puppy can be vital to our health and can improve quality of life.

*T*wenty-two years ago, Michael Shinabery, a radio and print journalist from New Mexico, was jogging in San Angelo, Texas, when his Doberman pinscher puppy, Midnight, struggled against his leash to pull him in the opposite direction.

"I stubbornly felt the dog should do what I wanted," Mike told us. "Within a short time, a tornado descended. The windows of the cars next to an apartment building I was near imploded. I was in a whirlwind, then a sudden calm before the frenzy erupted once again. If I'd only heeded the puppy's 'advice' I would not have ended up in the hospital emergency room with glass in one of my eyes."

We know Michael quite well, and we also know that he has listened to his dog's advice and profited from puppy love ever since.

Those of us who have shared our lives with dogs have found that some of life's greatest lessons have been taught to us by our puppies. With some pups, our time together may have been brief, and, sadly, they never had the opportunity of leaving puppyhood. Others reached maturity to meet the challenges of adulthood and to share many years of friendship, love, and loyalty.

On the following pages, coauthor Brad Steiger shares the "Six Great Life Lessons" that he learned from four remarkable puppies—Toby, Rex, Queen, and Reb.

Toby

*I*n the 1930s, it was a necessity on Iowa farms to have one or more dogs to help take care of livestock and to oversee the protection of the calves, pigs, chickens, and sheep against the nocturnal marauding of predators. When I was four years old, we had Old Bill, a big collie, to help round up the cattle and provide muscle against unwanted night visitors. Toby, our little black-and-white rat terrier, did his best to control the ever-multiplying rodent population that raided corn and oat bins and stole eggs from chicken houses.

I loved Old Bill and the security that his presence gave to our farm, but Toby was a fun-loving pup, just a few months old. Bill was getting along in years, losing his teeth, becoming a little grumpy and hard of hearing; playing with a little boy was no longer his idea of a good time. Toby, on the other hand, was always up for a romp on the lawn or in the fields. He wasn't avoiding his responsibilities when we ran in the pastures or the fields. He would always take time to sniff out a rabbit warren or a rat hole. Toby's skill at excavating rodent residences with his front paws, combined with the deadly prowess of his jaws and sharp teeth, often enabled him to bring home a trophy and receive praise from Dad, who hailed Toby as a tough, dependable, little bounty hunter.

There comes a time, however, when even the toughest and strongest should acknowledge that it is better to retreat and live to fight another day than to take on clearly impossible odds and die in the fray. In those days, so close to the Great Depression, with many people still feeling a residual financial pinch, some pet owners in the nearby towns and villages decided that they could no longer afford to feed their dogs or cats. In order to save money, many of these individuals loaded up their pets and drove them out to the gravel roads of the rural areas and dumped them, falsely assuming that there would always enough to eat for their cast-off pet on a farm. Because the farmers already had their dogs and a barn full of cats, they were faced with the unpleasant task of warding off the unwelcome invaders. Those dogs who escaped the farmers' shotguns formed dangerous and vicious packs that preyed on livestock. The cats who couldn't find a friendly hearth or a nourishing bowl of milk took to the woods and began to spawn generations of feral felines that shed all vestiges of domesticity.

In the spring of 1940, country folk faced the menace of roaming packs of dogs combined with the annual threat of rabies. Until the farmers in our area could eliminate the danger of the groups of killer canines and rabies season passed, Dad decided that Bill and Toby would have to spend their nights locked in the cob house, the old building near our house where we kept the corncobs we used in our kitchen cook stove. There was no way that he wanted the aging collie and the feisty rat terrier trying to ward off a pack of a dozen or more hounds that would range in size and breed from big German shepherds to medium-sized beagles and spaniels. Plus, there was the real possibility that one or more of these rogue animals would be rabid. One bite or scratch from a carrier of rabies would be enough to infect our dogs with the terrible madness of the disease.

Bill didn't mind spending the night lying on the cobs in the shed. He would hear the howls and barks of strange dogs prowling the farm, growl an obligatory warning, and then, his righteous anger expressed, he would settle back on the cobs and clear away an area for his bed. Toby, on the other hand, couldn't stand being locked in the shed when uninvited guests were rummaging around in the darkness of our farm. He wanted to get out of there and do some serious brawling with the night marauders. He was eleven pounds of danger, death, and destruction to those outlaws who dared to trespass on our farm.

Toby's misguided sense of bravado and his undeniable bravery proved to be his undoing. With those sharp teeth that had led to the demise of countless vermin, Toby chewed a hole through the wood door of the shed just large enough for him to squeeze through and challenge the pack of invaders.

It was easy for Dad to reconstruct the terrible events of the night when he approached the shed at first light of morning. Old Bill was whining his distress and frustration. It was obvious from the cuts and bloody wounds on his muzzle that he had tried to force himself through the tiny hole, in order to come to Toby's assistance. But Toby was gone. The hole he had chewed through the wooden door and the little red collar that had been ripped from around his neck was the only evidence to prove that he had ever existed.

Night after night for weeks afterward, I prayed that the courageous little terrier would return to us, but I knew with all my childish fervor that if Toby were alive, he would come back to me.

Puppy Miracles

Important Lesson Number One

One should strive to be brave, courageous, and bold, but one should not confuse these admirable virtues with bravado, recklessness, and impetuousness. Such confusion can, at the least, cause great embarrassment and humiliation—or in extreme instances, get you injured or killed.

Rex

Old Bill passed away not long after Toby disappeared. We tried to replace our fine dogs first with Moko, another rat terrier, who managed to live only a couple of months before a rabid raccoon bit him; and second, with a hound that didn't last long enough for him to earn a name other than "Long Ears" before he was bitten by a rabid skunk and had to be put down.

Then, Rex arrived on our farm. He was a robust, rusty-colored, mixed-breed pup with a bit of shepherd, a dash of Border collie, and a good helping of all-American mutt. I was eight years old, and it seemed obvious to me that the puppy should be named Rusty. However, Grandma Dena, who was the librarian in our Iowa village and the matriarch in our family, suggested that because of his regal bearing, I should name him Rex, which in Latin translates to *king*.

I found in the pup a great friend and a trusted confidant, who would listen with careful attention when I told him of my worries and concerns regarding my social interactions with my classmates. Rex came to our farm at a more propitious time than had Toby, Moko, or Long Ears had.

The marauding packs of dogs had greatly diminished in numbers because of the rifles and shotguns of farmers who had had enough of nighttime raids of the outlaw gangs carrying off their chickens and killing or maiming their cattle, sheep, and pigs. Rabies was still a very great danger, especially in the spring, but now it was becoming a bit more common for farmers to vaccinate their dogs.

My four-year-old sister June and I had been so inspired by our local veterinarian that we began hauling any crippled chicken, duck, or kitten to our hospital in the apple orchard. Here, in a shabby chicken coop that was no longer fit to house respectable laying hens, we nursed an assortment of injured creatures back to health.

One of our more successful patients was a tiny, undersized kitten that we named Pee Wee. He had come to us undersized, undernourished, and unsociable—hissing and clawing at our every attempt to help him. Over the course of several weeks, exercising considerable patience and lots of choice bits of food from our dinner plates, we had put some flesh on his bones and had managed to instill in him an attitude of reciprocal affection. His growls had been replaced with purrs; his slashing claws had been supplanted by body rubs against our legs. I would sit for hours playing with Pee Wee, holding a leaf for him to box, pretending a bit of cloth was a mouse in the grass for him to crouch, pounce, and grab. I found my circle of love growing to include my parents, my sister, Rex, and Pee Wee.

Then came the fateful afternoon that Pee Wee ventured from our hospital in the apple orchard to the house, filled with his new sense of confidence and well-being. Rex was in the house yard and had just been fed. I was so happy that my two best friends would finally meet. *How appropriate,* I thought, as Pee Wee approached Rex's bowl. They would begin their friendship by sharing a meal. In my naïve, eight-year-old reality concept, the three of us best friends would have many exciting adventures together on the farm.

I will never forget the images so clearly embedded in my memory and psyche for more than sixty years. Rex was wolfing down his food and seemed only peripherally aware that something was trying to edge its way into the perimeter of his dinner bowl. Barely taking a pause from his feeding, Rex swung his hungry muzzle to the side, seized Pee Wee by the neck, and tossed the kitten's tiny body into the air. Pee Wee was dead by the time he landed. Rex resumed eating, not in the slightest degree distracted from the pleasure of his meal by the momentary disturbance.

I ran to Pee Wee, grabbing up his limp body, crying his name through my tears, cradling him next to my chest as if my heartbeat could somehow restore his life force. I screamed my pain and outrage at Rex, who barely glanced up at me, but wagged his tail in response to my shouting his name in horror and disgust. Then, I struck the puppy who I had so loved—but who I now so hated and wished I had never met. Confused, completely baffled at my histrionics and my cruel interruption of his meal, Rex growled and showed his teeth in warning to back off and let him finish his dinner.

At that point, my mother and sister came out of the house to see what was causing such a ruckus in the front yard. I ran to them, shouting my anger with the vile Rex, the vicious monster who had so callously taken a life. Tearfully, I showed her Pee Wee's crumpled body in my hands. June saw his little corpse and began to scream and cry at the terrible deed that Rex had committed.

Mom sat down on the front porch steps and tried her best to comfort us and explain that it was not fair for us to judge dogs and cats by the Ten Commandments or by any of God's or people's laws. That evening at the supper table, Dad agreed with Mom and added that Rex had acted instinctively. He was only doing what comes naturally to a dog protecting his food, just the way that a dog thousands of years ago would have acted. Dad also pointed out that dogs and cats had not been getting along very well for many thousands of years, It was not very realistic of me to think that Pee Wee and Rex would have become buddies—especially considering their first ill-fated meeting was over Rex's dinner.

My intense hatred of Rex lasted only until the next morning when he eagerly awaited for me to finish my breakfast so we could get to work on our chores of the day. I hugged him and told him I loved him and that I understood that he didn't mean to kill Pee Wee. June and I held a brief service for Pee Wee later that day and buried him next to the lilac bushes.

Important Lesson Number Two

One must not judge dogs or any animals by human values, laws, or morals. Dogs are not junior humans seeking to become us. They are marvelous beings in their own right who must be judged on their own merits and abilities. Dogs wish our approval, not our judgment.

Important Lesson Number Three

Life is precious, and it can be taken from us in a split second. We must endeavor to live each moment to the fullest and to savor the blessings of family and friends.

Queen

*Q*ueen remains as one of the most complex and interesting personalities that I have ever known. Our family is seldom together for long before we begin sharing memories of Queen, the wild dog who came to love us and defend us.

In the spring of 1945, Rex was accidentally run over by a tractor driven by one of the hired hands Dad had employed to help with the planting. As if it weren't sad and terrible enough to lose Rex, that same spring a terrible plague of distemper decimated the dog population in northwestern Iowa. As a farm family who tilled 280 acres of corn, hay, oats, and soybeans; herded fifty head of cattle, about two hundred pigs, and a hundred or so chickens, ducks, and geese; we desperately required the services of a good dog. Months before the disease struck, there had been no shortage of folks trying to give puppies away at county fairs, at gas stations, and outside grocery stores on Saturday nights. After the disease spread, puppies were as scarce as white crows.

One day, a farmer who supplemented his income by trapping told us that he had come upon a wild collie and her litter of pups in the woods near the creek where he had his trap lines. The last time he had seen them, there was only one pup running with the mother. If we wanted a dog so desperately, he suggested, we could try to catch the wild pup. But he added that we had better hurry, because he intended to shoot them first chance he had to stop them from ruining his trapping by driving mink, muskrats, and fox away from the creek.

Under ordinary circumstances, farmers like our family would never have considered bringing a wild dog onto the homestead. A dog that has been born free and wild would be smarter, meaner, and more destructive than a normal domesticated canine. Foxes, coyotes, or wolves kill only what they need to survive, and they usually single out the old and the crippled from a herd of deer or elk. However, wild dogs often kill only for the sport, the fun of it—perhaps not unlike the human hunters from whom they have fled.

With the full understanding that we might never be able to fully domesticate the offspring of a wild dog, the four of us—Mom, Dad, June, and I—set out one afternoon, just before chore time, for the section of the woods where trappers and farmers had most often seen the outlaw collie and her pup. Although we tried our best to be as quiet as possible in our approach to the wild dogs' lair, the big white collie emerged and cautiously watched us as we approached. When we were about twenty yards from the hideout, the mother gave a yelp of warning and the two of them set off running.

"Let's get the pup!" Dad shouted. "Run it down!"

We ran through the woods at top speed, but I am certain that we never would have caught our prize if we hadn't cornered the snarling pup against an old rusted wire fence. Although a mother dog will fight to the death to defend her young pups, this one must have considered the pup to be old enough to fend for itself, because the mother kept right on running without looking back.

Dad took off his leather belt, looped it tight around the dog's snapping jaws, and quickly assessed our potential new pup. It was female, probably a white collie-shepherd mix, and about five or six months old. Dad grumbled that she might have enjoyed too much of the wild and free life to ever settle down for us. We'd probably never be able to train her, and she might eat our chickens and our piglets.

After several minutes of serious deliberation concerning the pup's ultimate fate, Dad and Mom decided that our desperate need for a dog outweighed all negative considerations. Dad wrapped the snarling, struggling pup in the worn Indian blanket that we always kept in the back seat of our old Chevy and carried her back with us to our farm.

The couple of weeks that followed were awful. We had to keep the wild pup locked in the cob house to keep her from running back to the woods and the wild life. She was vicious. It seemed as though she never stopped snarling, snapping, and trying to bite us. She wouldn't eat for days, and trying to coax her to take a bite of food was interpreted by the pup as an opportunity to take a bite out of your hand.

Whether it was having starved before or realizing that food could be available on a regular basis, she began to accept the food that we offered her. For several weeks more, it was still one step at a time. I received more than one painful bite to my fingers when I attempted to pet her before she was ready to receive a touch from any of us.

I don't think we ever thought of calling her anything other than Queen. With her haughty, imperious, no-nonsense manner, no other name would have been appropriate.

The family unanimously decided to keep Queen, and we agreed that she should wear a collar with a dog license

Puppy Miracles

around her neck. We decided Dad would be the one to put the collar on.

His first attempt brought the expected snarl and a warning growl to back off. Then Dad began to speak in a cheerful enthusiastic voice about how pretty she would look with the collar around her neck. We all laughed at his thinking *this* dog—the wildest dog we knew—would understand the human concept of beauty.

Dad kept up the mantra of "beauty in a collar" and urged *us* to tell Queen how spiffy she would look when she wore it. It became a kind of game for us, joining Dad's chorus of persuasion and singing the praises of the magnificent leather collar with the tag on it.

Strangely enough, to all of our astonishment, Queen ceased snarling and permitted Dad to fasten the collar around her neck. Fully believing that she would snap and snarl and run around the barnyard until she managed to rip the noose from her neck, my mouth dropped open in awe as Queen actually seemed to preen, strutting back and forth in front of us.

"Look how pretty she is!" Dad pronounced, and we all echoed our agreement of her beauty as group reinforcement. "Queen is so pretty in her spiffy new collar!"

From that moment on, it was impossible to touch her collar under any circumstances. Even playfully suggesting that one might wish to borrow her collar or to try it on would invite a warning growl.

Although she would toil side by side with us, she would never accept any of our efforts to "train" her. When completing chores, Queen seemed to know, by some seemingly supernatural ability, what was required of her and she would carry out the task to the best of her ability. Because she always seemed to feel that she was fulfilling her end of any chore, she would not tolerate any form of correction or criticism. To attempt to scold Queen for an action we deemed a misdeed prompted a snarl and a warning growl in return.

In the years to come, Queen worked with us in the fields, herded cattle, nearly froze to death with us in blizzards rounding up livestock, defended us against wild dogs, and did chores with us every morning and night. Queen was never "just a dog." She was always Queen, an individual, independent being who chose of her own volition to be our friend, our partner, our coworker, our fully accepted family member. Queen will always remain in my memory as an individual as unique as any human being with whom I have shared deep and meaningful experiences. As I grow older, I appreciate even more the marvelous opportunity that my family was given by sharing our lives with a four-legged sovereign entity who always demanded that she be accepted as an equal on her own terms—and yet who came to give of herself unselfishly and completely.

Important Lesson Number Four

Dogs must be respected for who and what they are: Sovereign entities who possess an individual personality and their own rightful share of the Divine Spirit, whose breath gives life to all things. Dogs are not slavish underlings dependent upon humans. Dogs experience the world differently from humans, and their own special awareness and spiritual qualities give them a unique purpose in the universe.

Reb

Reb came to our family from the streets of Chicago. I was no longer a child, but thirty-five years old with four children of my own, ranging in age from thirteen to five. I should have been strong enough to turn away the puppy who followed a young boy home to his apartment in the Windy City's Old Town. Rosemarie, an actress and mother of the young boy, explained over the telephone that the beagle pup was collarless, therefore, tracing the owner was impossible. She already had two sons and one of the largest cats in the western world, so she decided that Reb (as she named him) would be a perfect fit in our rural home. I was less than enthusiastic to learn that Rosemarie's older son was already packing the car for the long drive to northeastern Iowa to deliver Reb to our doorstep, hearth, and home.

All my fears about a city pup adjusting to country living vanished the moment Reb came walking into our front room wagging his tail with the ease of a natural charmer. His alert, merry eyes seemed to say, "Hello, folks. I really hope you like me because I can sense that we were made for each other."

The entire family seemed to share Reb's feelings that we were in the presence of such an extraordinary personality. It was as if each of us could achieve almost instant rapport on a mental level with this incredibly charming puppy who was about seven or eight months old. I found myself speaking to him as if he were a newly arrived house guest capable of understanding my every word. "Hello, Reb. You may enter the kitchen, because the floor has indoor-outdoor carpeting. Your bowls for food and water are in the porch just off the kitchen. Please do not enter the living room because of the new carpeting that will pick up your loose hair. You have access to the upstairs, and your bed is in the large basket on the second-floor landing."

It was that simple. And I never had to repeat my instructions.

I remember the time when an editor friend of mine from New York was visiting us during a week of celebration in our little Iowa community. My children and their mother (Marilyn, who died in 1982) had already left to march in the big parade, so my friend and I trailed a bit behind, busily engaged in conversation. We had walked about a block from our house when I became aware of Reb following quietly behind us.

"Oh, Reb," I said in a quite, apologetic voice, "I am so sorry, but you cannot come along on this walk. We are going downtown where there will be crowds of people. You would not be comfortable in such noise and hubbub. Please go back to the front steps and wait for us there. I promise we won't be long."

Reb listened to my explanation, then, satisfied with its truthfulness and sincerity, turned and walked back to the front steps to await our return.

My editor's eyes were wide with amazement. "That was incredible," he said. "You spoke to your dog just as you do to your children. And he obeyed just as well. You didn't gesture. You didn't point. You didn't raise your voice. It was as if he understood every word that you spoke to him."

"Why not?" I joked. "Reb was born in this country, too!"

Further, Reb was an unusually alert watchdog. He was on the case any time of the day or night. Unsolicited visitors arriving on our property would be unable to leave their vehicles unless one of our family members authorized Reb to back off.

Even more impressive was Reb's uncanny ability to perceive, who among complete strangers to him, were known to the family. Reb seemed to know if the occupant of the strange automobile was an old high school classmate I hadn't seen for twenty years or a cousin I had not seen since a family reunion ten years before. Somehow aware of my prior relationship with that person, Reb would approach the vehicle without growling or barking his usual warning to strangers. Instead, he would wag his tail in a friendly manner and cheerily usher the visitor to our front door.

While the skeptics may quickly argue that I provided visual clues of acceptance when the visitors arrived that the alert beagle sensed, I will stress the fact that I was always inside the house, most often working at my typewriter, while Reb was outside, alone with our unexpected guests. How our remarkable beagle could somehow ascertain who of the strangers were friends or relatives and who were truly uninvited visitors presently remains a mystery to our methods of scientific analysis.

Important Lesson Number Five

There is a blessed Oneness with all life, and it is possible to establish a beautiful, perhaps limitless, mind-link with all creatures that will allow you to gain a fuller understanding of the mysteries of God's continuing acts of creation. When you make a true, spiritual connection with your dog, you recognize that you are both individual expressions of the Divine and both spiritual beings in the Oneness.

*H*ave you ever wondered what you might do for your puppy if you wanted to give him or her a special reward for its loyalty, its love, its affection? Perhaps if you were a dentist, you might give your puppy a gold tooth. That is what Dr. Milan Vujnovic from Banja Luka, Bosnia, did for his eight-month-old Russian terrier Atos, to show his appreciation for the pup's loyalty.

Dr. Vujnovic said that Atos likes the gold tooth gleaming in his mouth and the dog knows that it is special. According to the dentist, Atos even shows the gold tooth off to people because he knows that it is something special to see in a dog's mouth. Even though the process of placing the gold tooth in his mouth took four hours, Atos sat stoically through the whole procedure and didn't move an inch.

The Russian terrier, Dr. Vujnovic asserts, is the most intelligent of all dogs, and it can also be one of the fiercest. The dentist said that he has no worries about thieves attempting to steal Atos' tooth, for Russian terriers are descended from the special dogs used by the Soviet KGB, the secret police. Atos would *never* allow a petty thief to steal anything from *him*!

*W*hen Eliza Hastings acquired Lulu, an eight-month-old Labrador, she may have been hoping that she would grow to be a really terrific watchdog. However, Lulu became a "watchdog" of a different kind when she ate Eliza's $2,000 Gucci watch, a very special Christmas present from her husband, Richard.

Eliza and Richard were hosting overnight guests at their home in Pamington, Tewkesbury, UK, and Eliza had made certain that the doggy gate at the bottom of the stairs was closed, because, as she told a reporter from *The Citizen*, their lady visitor had very nice shoes and she didn't want Lulu slipping upstairs while they were having dinner and chewing on them. "Lulu has a passion for chewing things," Eliza explained.

Later in the evening, Eliza noticed that the doggy gate had somehow been opened, and she feared the worst. A quick trip upstairs and a peek in the guest bedroom assured her that all was well with their guest's expensive shoes.

It was when the guests and the Hastingses had retired to their respective bedrooms that Eliza discovered that her Gucci watch was missing from her dresser table. Remembering that she had found the doggy gate open earlier that evening, Eliza said that she had a "feeling, almost a sixth sense," that her watch's disappearance had something to do with Lulu.

Richard and Eliza brought their Labrador to the Arvonia Animal Hospital and explained their suspicions to veterinarian Dr. Richard Hillam. An X-ray confirmed their theory that Lulu had gobbled the Gucci.

Dr. Hillam decided to operate in order to restore the watch to Eliza's possession and to relieve Lulu's stomach of any contents lacking nutritional value. First, the veterinarian removed a very large sock, which proved rather difficult to remove. Next, he extricated the Gucci watch, which had taken a licking, but was still ticking. Lulu's potent gastric juices had tarnished the watch's metal case a bit, and the strap was partially chewed, but the Gucci still showed perfect time.

In spite of the watch's retrieval and its sound working order, Eliza told reporters that she did not intend to wear it again, being very aware of where it had been. Describing Lulu's temperament for the press, Eliza emphasized that the puppy was a lovely dog with a lovely disposition, but disposed to indulge her unusual appetites. Lulu had previously swallowed socks, dice, and, Eliza added, "She would have eaten my mother's engagement ring had I not heard it rattling around in her mouth."

Lulu is not alone in her bizarre dietary cravings. In *More Strange Powers of Pets,* we recounted the stories of a Labrador-Newfoundland-mix puppy that swallowed a nine-inch carving knife, a Border collie that gulped a twelve-inch cake knife, a Great Dane that gobbled the cue ball from a pool table, and a 60-pound guard dog that downed a $15,000 diamond ring.

Not long ago, we learned of Darwin, a sad-eyed beagle puppy, who had swallowed his owner's engagement ring.

Becky said that she had never taken the ring off her finger since her fiancé, Rick, had placed it there. But on this one occasion, she had taken it off for just a moment and placed it in her shirt pocket. A few minutes later she wished to return the symbol of love to her finger to discover—horror of horrors, *it was not in her pocket!* As if she had tempted fate by removing it just that one time, Rick's engagement ring had disappeared.

After she had conducted a thorough search of the area where the ring would have fallen from her shirt pocket, her female intuition told Becky that Darwin, her twelve-week-old beagle puppy, had something to do with the ring's mysterious disappearance.

An X-ray at the veterinarian's office confirmed Becky's hunch. Darwin had spotted the shiny object on the floor and had obviously decided that it was meant to be a special treat for extra good beagles such as himself.

Becky and Rick stuffed Darwin with high-fiber puppy biscuits in order to help *move* his digestive process along. Within a couple of days, Darwin passed the ring—and after a good cleaning, the ring was as good as new.

When Abby, a one-year-old golden retriever, swallowed a rubber ball, it looked as though she truly had bitten off more than she could chew.

Rita Fisler was out walking her own dog in her neighborhood in Boston when she saw her friend, Mike Gorman, kneeling beside Abby. A normally energetic canine, Abby was lying still on the ground. A distraught Gorman told Rita that at first he thought Abby was playing, but then he realized that she wasn't breathing. She had

Puppy Miracles

swallowed her rubber ball, and he could tell that she needed help *fast*.

Lucky for Abby, Rita had just completed a CPR course. If those techniques worked for humans, she reasoned, why not for a golden retriever?

She picked up the limp dog and began performing the Heimlich maneuver on Abby.

At first nothing happened, but the determined Rita refused to quit. Then, the elated Gorman saw the ball shoot out of Abby's mouth as if it were fired from the barrel of a rifle.

Within minutes, thanks to Rita Fisler's determined application of her CPR training, Abby was once again bounding about—and wanting to chase after the same rubber ball that had almost choked her to death.

Some years ago, while Sherry was browsing through a flea market in Phoenix, Arizona, she encountered a couple at one of the stalls who had allowed their Lhasa Apso puppy to become unhealthily obese. Noting her interest in their dog, whose tummy almost touched the ground, one of the owners told her that they were going to have the puppy put to sleep because it was nothing but a little garbage disposal. Sherry took pity on the little dog and said that she would take him home with her rather than let him face an executioner.

The couple handed the Lhasa Apso's leash to her, told her that she was welcome to him, and said good riddance to a puppy whom Sherry would christen Simba, *lion*, to start building his self-respect. With her nutritional background and her interest in health and physical conditioning, Sherry was confident that she would be able to rehabilitate the barely walking, fur-covered bowling ball into a slimmer new doggy. She put Simba on a diet and managed to whittle him down from disgustingly obese to pleasingly plump. Of course, that didn't mean that the fuzzy little gourmand did not prove with each passing day that eating was still his favorite pastime; plus, he had to be watched continually. Rattle a pan in the kitchen, and like magic, Simba appears.

Once when Brad was making dinner, he wiped his hands on a paper towel and accidentally dropped it as he moved a pan on the counter.

The towel never reached the floor. To Brad's amazement, the ever-hungry Simba, who had been watching his every move as he prepared the evening meal, caught the wet, wadded paper sheet and swallowed it in one contented gulp.

Fearing that the little dog would surely choke on such a large paper towel, Brad got down on his knees and pried open Simba's mouth with his fingers, hoping to catch the tail of the towel and pull it out of his throat.

There was not a trace of the towel to be seen. It had cleared Simba's teeth and throat and been immediately pulled down to his gullet. Not only was he not choking or gasping at any kind of impediment lodged in his throat, his tail was wagging happily, as if asking for another helping of soggy towel à la Brad. None the worse for wear, Simba impatiently awaited the serving of his more traditional, nutritional dinner.

Puppies' tummies, it seems, are meant to be able to digest nearly anything that can passed between its jaws. This does not mean that one should encourage one's pup to develop the unwise habit of scarfing down everything in sight. One should always strive to create healthful and nutritional dietary habits as early in the puppy's life as possible.

*I*t was every parent's worst nightmare. On Labor Day 1992, John and Sheila Morrison decided to treat their pretty eleven-year-old daughter Rachel to a roller coaster ride at an amusement park in Grand Prairie, Texas. As the ride's car whipped around a bend, Rachel was thrown out. In horror, the Morrisons watched helplessly as their daughter plummeted to the ground twenty-five feet below.

The doctors were not optimistic, and their words were far from encouraging. The Morrisons were informed that their daughter had suffered severe brain damage.

The tragic bottom line was that she might not live. And if she did, the medical experts warned, she might spend the rest of her life in a vegetative state.

On October 7, Rachel began undergoing pet therapy at the Baylor Institute for Rehabilitation in Dallas. The director of the program, Shari Bernard, brought a number of dogs to the comatose girl, and Rachel slowly began to respond to a few simple commands.

Although striving to remain positive, it was sadly apparent that the child's responses were scarcely more than robotic and that she still gave little evidence that she was in touch with her environment. Most often, Rachel would simply sit still in her wheelchair, mute and unresponsive.

Then, on October 14, Shari brought Belle, a lively Australian sheepdog puppy to Rachel's side.

Slowly, Rachel reached out to put her arm around Belle.

Shari said that Australian sheepdogs have no tails, then she asked Rachel which doggy part was Belle missing.

Rachel suddenly whispered, "A tail."

Shari Bernard could barely hear those first softly uttered words, but she was certain that she had heard Rachel break her long silence.

She admitted that she was stunned. It was as if the puppy had somehow been able to penetrate the deep recesses of the child's consciousness and enable her to speak again. Rachel's first words since Labor Day came out very slowly, forced from deep within her.

That evening, to the unrestrained joy of Sheila Morrison, she was able to speak to her daughter on the telephone.

Shari Bernard told reporters that in the eight years that she had worked in pet therapy at the Baylor Institute for Rehabilitation, she had never witnessed a case quite so dramatic as that of Rachel's. "It was as if there was a special bond between Belle and Rachel," she said.

Rachel, who continued to make steady progress, said simply, "I love being with dogs. Belle made me want to speak again."

parky is a Border collie puppy that will one day join Radar, Jet, and the others on the job at Southwest Florida International Airport (SWFIA) in Fort Myers, Florida. You might ask, what job does a Border collie have at an airport? An extremely important job would be the answer airport management would give—a job of keeping the runways clear of birds.

Before they began using the dogs, SWFIA had averaged nearly twenty collisions a year with birds on the runways. Once, a close encounter with a sand hill crane even resulted in an emergency aircraft landing.

In 1999, Jet became the first Border collie air traffic controller and the statistic dropped from twenty bird collisions to just six a year. Jet put in two years of outstanding service at the airport, but early in 2001, she was diagnosed with a degenerative heart condition and the veterinarian advised an early retirement from runway patrol.

Jet's successor was Radar, another Border collie and a graduate of the Flyaway Farm and Kennels in Reidsville, North Carolina. Her human coworkers immediately declared Radar to be superb at her job.

Although Border collies generally weigh no more than thirty pounds, the breed is recognized as one of the most intelligent. SWFIA personnel consider the small dogs perfectly capable of being responsible for looking after aircraft that often weigh many tons. SWFIA was the first commercial airport in the United States to begin using Border collies to keep the runways clear of birds. Other airports had used falcons or other birds of prey to swoop down on the feathered trespassers and carry them off, but SWFIA personnel are convinced that their solution is more humane.

Border collies have been bred for centuries for their ability to herd sheep and geese without inflicting any harm upon animals. SWFIA personnel believe that this instinct to herd without hurting makes them ideal for protecting the straying wildlife as well. From sunrise to sunset, the Border collies merely chase away the birds that have wandered onto the runways—never stopping to make a snack out of them.

Puppy Miracles

*J*anice Gray Kolb, author of such inspirational books about pets and people as *Solace of Solitude—Afterlife Visits: A Journey* shared the following episode in the rearing of her six children and countless puppies.

"During the wonderful years spent raising our six children, we also had the privilege of being the caring companions of three little Cairn terriers. Two of them shared life with us for sixteen years and another for seventeen. All three enriched each one of us in an abundance of ways.

"Eliza Brehon (Lizzie) was born in Ireland, and we acquired her at three months of age complete with her lovely name. A year later she had four adorable puppies sired by a Cairn terrier champion—two of which we kept. Lizzie, Muffin, and Crackers accompanied us on all our family vacations. For safety, we kept the dogs inside a large pen as we drove, occasionally letting the puppies out to cuddle with our children.

"From our home in Pennsylvania, these little dogs motored all over the country and into Canada, joining us on our weekend camping trips. They were a part of us and because of them, we talked with many strangers who were delighted with our little dogs and whom we never would have met without our canine ambassadors.

"Of all our vacations with these dear little terriers, it is one in the summer of 1972 that sticks out in our minds. The night before we were to leave for the cottage we had rented for two weeks on Lake Winnipesaukee in Wolfeboro, New Hampshire, Muffin could not be found.

"Since all three dogs were always in our home or fenced in yard, how she escaped was a mystery. Distraught and worried, two of my daughters and I went to our basement to check out some strange sounds we had heard. Upon moving a piece of furniture we found what appeared to be a wet ball of crying fur. Although we had personally delivered puppies in the past, we were blinded to the fact that it might possibly be a puppy because none of our dogs were expecting. Wrong! Muffin's normal chunkiness, which was part of her charm, concealed her pregnancy, which had gone undetected by us all.

"Soon, we found a total of six crying newborn puppies in the basement with their mother. This was a miracle to us, for we remembered the extreme difficulty Muffin's mother had had giving birth to her and her three siblings. Lizzie had been frightened, and needed and wanted our assistance for all four births. We had rented a whelping pen and carefully monitored during her labor, and then aided in the four deliveries.

"To realize our young Muffin had gone through six births alone without our help was heartbreaking. Having given birth to six babies myself—of course, not all at once and with a doctor attending—I had such love, admiration, and sympathy for her and her courage.

"After caring for all six puppies, we knew we still had to go ahead with our vacation plans. Our entire family looked forward to these two weeks for months.

"The next morning, our van cruised north to New Hampshire containing two parents, six children, and nine dogs. Close friends could not comprehend how we could leave. We knew from past experience that somehow all would be well.

"The six babies proved to be no trouble, for their mother, Muffin, took total responsibility. The puppies spent the two weeks confined to a very large, empty child's swimming pool in the cottage. Their mother spent much time in there with them for feedings and for general comfort. Lizzie and Crackers kept a devoted watch near the pool.

What seemed to others an insane adventure proved to be a cherished memory.

When animal companions are permitted to share our lives to the fullest, it is then that unconditional love, joy, consolation, and unexpected rewards and surprises will be experienced—not to mention miracles. What greater miracle than new life?

"In the weeks that followed our vacation, the time came to find new homes for the puppies. Those interested had to come to our home where we could learn about the puppies and their life styles. We made the prospective owners promise that if they no longer wanted to keep the puppy they would return it to us. Very quickly, all six puppies were placed in loving homes, and the owners kept in touch with us throughout each puppy's lifetime, occasionally sending us pictures. This in itself was a miracle of love, and it was clear the families loved each puppy very much. Those precious creatures were pure gifts.

"We are truly grateful for the long years we shared love, home, and itinerary with our three Cairn terriers who came to us in the preciousness and God-given miracle of puppyhood."

*O*ur friend, syndicated columnist Terri Schlichenmeyer, has a theory. "I believe that, if you have a very beloved dog—one you've had for years and that you're very close to—when he dies, he goes to God before he goes over the famed Rainbow Bridge. I believe that he helps God choose your next dog. He whispers secrets in that new pup's ear, telling him who to look for and what to remember when he gets here. Your new dog isn't going to show up in your life until you're ready, but when he does, you can be sure he's the dog you were supposed to have."

Terri continued with a story to illustrate her theory of how your beloved, dearly departed dog works with a Higher Power to bring a new puppy into your life.

"I had a terrier named Smedley that I got even before I married David, my late husband. He watched over us while David was sick with cancer, and he mourned with me when Dave died. Smedley was patient with me when I started dating again, through bad dates and good ones. He met Jim and was again patient with me when Jim and I got married. When I got cancer myself, Smedley "took care" of me.

"In 1992, Smedley got sick and we had to ease his transition to God. I'm sure the spirits of David and Smedley started looking for a new pup for me right away.

"Our little Muffin, another terrier who was Smedley's companion, hated to be left alone, so we started thinking about getting another small pup to be with her. Every one we saw was either too big or too aggressive. Every dog we saw was just, somehow, *wrong.*

"In May of 1994, I was at our local Humane Society, looking again. That very morning, two college girls had dropped off a Lhasa apso, saying that they couldn't care for him any more and that the landlord wanted him gone. I went back in the dog room to have a look.

"The second I opened the door, this little fur ball threw himself at the kennel door and howled for me. He was six months old and parti-colored, his hair askew. But he was cute as the dickens.

"I opened the kennel door and pulled him out. He wrapped his little legs around my arm, put his little head in my hand and cried like he couldn't believe I had finally found him . . . and I had never seen him before in my life.

"I snuggled him for a minute, and with permission, I took him out on a leash to gauge his temperament. He was a happy little guy, and I decided that this one had more than a just few possibilities. I took him back inside.

"When I put him back in the kennel, he howled, and cried, and carried on like he didn't want me to leave him. It nearly tore my heart out. I went back to the front desk and said, 'That Lhasa—that's *my* dog.'

'Oh, no,' they said. 'He was surrendered this morning.'

'No. You don't understand. That dog is *mine*. He chose me, and I'll take him.'

"The next day, we brought Muffin to the kennel to see if they would get along, and even though she didn't appear to think much of him, we thought we'd give it the weekend to decide. We brought the new puppy and named him Truman because it seemed to fit him. "He was a dignified little guy and won Muffy's friendship overnight.

"Muffin herself went to whisper secrets to God a few years ago. Truman is now twelve years old.

"I'd say that Smedley chose the right pup for me."

Completing her account of how Truman came into her life, Terri said that she wished to clear up some misconceptions about Lhasa apsos.

"If you read any of what the dog books say about Lhasas, you'll notice that experts claim that Lhasas aren't good with children," she began. "Lucky for me, Truman hasn't ever read those books."

When her nephew Eric was about four months old, Terri offered to babysit him one afternoon.

"It was a hot day, and Eric was fussy, so I put him in his bouncy-seat on the floor and set him in front of the fan," she said. "Muffin wasn't at all interested in children, and she crawled up on the couch. I wasn't sure what Truman would do. At the time, he was only about nine months old, and I had never seen him around babies.

"I watched carefully. Truman circled Eric once or twice. Eric noticed Truman and followed him with his eyes. Truman sniffed at Eric's cheek. Eric giggled. Truman kissed the baby. Eric giggled. Then I watched, amazed, as they began playing! Truman would lick Eric's feet and wait as Eric kicked and squealed. Truman walked to another spot, licked Eric's hand and waited as Eric waved his fingers and squealed. They played this game for about a half hour until finally, my nephew fell asleep.

"I had a perfect babysitting helper, and Eric had a new playmate!" Terri said, concluding her evidence for kid-friendly Lhasa apsos.

*L*ori Jean Flory, a spiritual medium and author of *The Wisdom Teachings of Archangel Michael*, which has provided inspiration and guidance for thousands of readers, shared with us the story of her collie Stormy, who Lori believes passed away and was reincarnated as their next puppy.

"It is my intention that this story might uplift those who have also lost beloved pets. My husband Charles and I think all dogs, cats, and all of our animal friends come as four-legged angels. Animals do have guides and guardian angels around them just as we do. They also have bodies of light, just as we do. And when they pass over, they continue in their bodies of light in the heavenly realms, just as we do. There are special angels who care for them and love them.

"Our animal friends are highly evolved spiritual beings in their own right. They are also individuals who have feelings, emotions, and thoughts.

"I often speak telepathically with them, and it's surprising some of the things they think. They come with spiritual lessons to learn and to teach their human friends. They are love on four paws.

"Stormy (or Pinewynd's Spring Storm, as Stormy's pedigree papers would have it), a tri-colored (black, white, and tan) collie came to this earth as a blessing from May 25, 1987 to August 13, 1994, a little over seven years. He had lymphatic cancer, problems with heart, lungs, respiratory, dehydration, as well as, I think, diabetes. He taught us much in his illness.

"When Charles and I moved up into the Colorado Mountains, we did not know Stormy was ill. One evening, not long after we had moved into our house, I felt his glands and they felt as large as golf balls. We called the vet and rushed him over for treatment.

"That was when the roller coaster began. For six or seven weeks, while Charles worked, I took Stormy to the vet twenty-six times, and his care became my twenty-four-hour-a-day project. An entire kitchen counter was devoted to his special diet and medications that had to be taken at different times and in different amounts and coordinated.

I was up every two hours taking his temperature and giving him an injection just under the skin. Sleep was a thing of the past.

"Sometimes Stormy would get better, and then he would nose dive, teaching us the gifts of little "feel good" miracles, as I came to call them. He had X-rays, EKGs—tests of every kind. He would be hooked up to tubes injecting electrolytes, and I would sometimes sit for hours and hold his paws or cradle his head.

"After this had been going on for quite awhile, we realized we were running out of money. We faced a difficult choice of continuing the expensive medical treatments and losing our house or letting Stormy go. I remember calling Charles at work that day, hysterical. We both decided together that it was time to let Stormy go, that he had no quality of life left, and by this time, was miserable. He had suffered so much pain. His eyes were dark and hollow. He had trouble getting up and would not come when called. For him, being released was a gift.

"Charles was in Denver at the time, and we agreed to meet up so we could take Stormy to the vet together. The whole ride down, Stormy lay depressed in the back seat. When we got near the vet's office, he started to lick Charles' face. Stormy knew relief was near.

Once we arrived, Charles and my emotions took over. We both began to cry so hard in the vet's lobby that we could not speak for minutes. In between sobs, we explained again to the clinic's staff what the situation was. They led us into a room, and we both kissed Stormy's nose. We said goodbye, and asked him to let us know he was okay once he was in spirit. We stayed a while longer, and when Stormy was gone, we went home. We could already feel his relief.

"As soon we got home, we both saw a bright, white light flash over Stormy's usual spot on the couch. Then a picture of an angel that was securely tacked to the wall fell to the floor. When we went to bed, I saw Stormy's face, now in spirit, hovering near the ceiling. I felt his presence at the side of the bed.

"The next morning, I heard a dog bark next to the bed when our other two dogs were upstairs. 'Stormy,' I said, 'we love you deeply and you will always be family to us no matter what. If you are ready to go into the light now, we will be okay. We will always be connected. We will always love you.'

"I received major resistance to that suggestion. Stormy was not yet ready to go. I heard, saw, sensed, and felt him on the inner and outer levels. He kept letting me know that he was coming back. When Charles and I were watching a *Lassie* movie, an intense wave of energy came over me and I *knew* that he was back that day.

"At night, I would dream of Stormy trying to get across a bridge to me or crawling through a window, attempting to come back. We knew that Stormy wanted to return to us, but we really had a hard time finding collie puppies in the state of Colorado. We used to show collies and had many contacts, but our search kept turning up fruitless. Finally, one Sunday evening I was looking in the ad section, and 'lo and behold, there they were: *collie puppies*. We couldn't exactly afford $250 for a puppy, but I convinced Charles to call, even though it was a couple hours' drive from us. They had but one female puppy left, and they promised to hold her for us until the next day.

"When we went to see the puppy, we fell in love with her right away. And to confirm my feelings that this was the dog for us, I saw a vision of Stormy's face right above her—and then his essence merged with that of the puppy's. I knew that he had come back. Almost immediately, the puppy began to do things that Stormy used to do that only we could recognize. We knew that we had been blessed and given another chance to be together again. Her AKC registration name is Cherie Star Bright Angel, and we named her Cherie.

"If you take away one thing from this story, let it be the knowledge that pets *do* move into the light just as we do— and sometimes, they come back. If not, when you make the transition someday, that beloved pet will be there to meet you. *Love lives on!*"

*I*f you happened to hear the Harris family of Hadnall, Shropshire, England, call their Labrador puppy a "Little Ding-a-Ling," you should hear the real story behind the nickname.

Beverly Harris had searched the household for days, wondering desperately how her cherished ornamental bell could have disappeared.

She had quizzed her husband Richard and their kids to determine if they had moved the bell from its usual place as some kind of joke, but they all swore that they were innocent of any prank.

Beverly felt that she would never see her precious bell again. It had simply vanished under mysterious circumstances. She could not imagine a burglar who would have broken into their home to take the ornamental bell and nothing else.

After a week, Beverly heard the bell's familiar ring as she was putting Hector to bed. The little scamp must somehow have taken the bell, brought it to his bed and hidden it with his other toys. Beverly went through the puppy's bedding, but did not find her bell.

Again, she heard the bell ringing. All at once, Beverly realized that the ringing was originating from the Labrador's stomach. She picked up Hector and gave him a little shake.

The bell sounded loud and clear. As incredible as it may seem, the puppy had swallowed her precious ornamental bell. Apparently, it had taken several days before the bell was positioned in Hector's stomach, allowing the ring to be heard when the pup was shaken.

Richard laughed until the tears ran down his cheeks. The Harris children also had a good chuckle at the pup *who rang* when he followed them around the house. They nicknamed Hector 'Tinkler' because the bell inside his stomach would ring whenever his movements shook it.

The Harrises knew that there was no way that the bell would be able to pass through a six-month-old puppy's intestinal track, and it was too well situated in the stomach for Hector to be able to vomit it up. They took "Tinkler" to veterinarian Dean Halligan, who told them that they were correct to bring the pup in. It the bell had worked its way into Hector's small intestine, Halligan said, it would have killed him.

Halligan could not help being amused. When he picked Hector up and shook him, the veterinarian commented that the pup sounded like a wind chime.

Perhaps the Harrises did not see the humor in the $600 price tag for the surgery to cut the ornamental bell free of Hector's stomach, but they now had the precious bell *and* their priceless puppy—both in one piece. As a bonus, the veterinarian found several garden stones that the little Labrador had swallowed too.

*T*he Portuguese towns of Sobrado and Ermesinde share a most unusual puppy mystery. One morning at 7:30 A.M. mass, a small black puppy wandered into the church in Ermesinde and looked around at the assembled parishioners and the priest standing before the altar. A couple of men tried to catch the puppy and send it outside, but it evaded them and ran down the aisle until it reached the altar. There it stopped, sat down, and appeared to be waiting for the priest to continue the service. The priest smiled, made a small comment about St. Francis and his love of animals, and continued with his sermon.

After the service was concluded, the puppy ran out the front door, skillfully avoiding all attempts to pet or deter it. The priest asked who, among his congregation, owned the dog, but no one claimed to have seen the black puppy who suddenly materialized in church.

To the amazement of the entire congregation at the next Sunday's early mass, the black puppy once again appeared at the church door and walked down the aisle to take a position next to the altar. This strange stray's routine continued for several weeks. Precisely at 7:30 A.M., the little black dog would appear, walk down the aisle, and sit by the altar. When the assembled worshippers stood, so would the dog. When they sat, the pup would follow the order of service exactly.

Eventually, someone in the neighboring town of Sabrado heard about the mysterious little dog and decided to give the stray pooch a home. He named the female puppy, Preta, Portuguese for *black*. Preta seemed happy to have an attentive owner who generously provided room and board. However, Preta's new companion was not a churchgoer.

Not one to press her religious views on her kind benefactor, Preta arose at 5:00 A.M. every Sunday morning to walk sixteen miles, so that she would be on time for mass in the Ermesinde church.

According to the newspaper *Correio da Manha*, the devout and dedicated Preta has made the Sunday morning pilgrimage for three years. After the service is concluded,

Preta walks back to her home in Sobrado. On occasion, she will accept a ride from a parishioner she knows. Otherwise, Preta treks back to Sobrado by herself, without complaint.

According to the priest in Ermsinde, the number of parishioners in his congregation has grown, because people want to see for themselves the truth of the story of Preta—and to worship along side this most religious canine.

At first, Lori Barnabe, an Animal Control Officer and Veterinary Technician at the Oakland (California) Animal Shelter, could not believe her eyes. The quivering tar ball in front of her was actually a three-month-old German shepherd–Labrador puppy, which had wandered into the middle of a work site and had been sprayed with hot tar.

Lori told a reporter that in spite of experiencing what must have been terrible pain, the dog looked up at her with big, sweet eyes that completely stole her heart.

Upon her examination of the pup, Lori found that he had suffered third-degree burns to all four paws, his knees, and back. But the pup, nicknamed Sparky by the shelter staff, still managed to wag his tail in appreciation for the kind treatment.

Sparky was transferred to Hopalong Animal Rescue, a non-profit organization that specializes in the rescue, rehabilitation, and placement of abused animals. A tragic case such as Sparky's might cost Hopalong as much as $4,500 in medical care, which would be paid for by public donations. Animals that have suffered a great deal of pain and suffering are also likely to have undergone severe emotional trauma and would have to be fully rehabilitated for several months before they can be placed in a loving, permanent home.

It was a miracle that a three-month-old puppy survived being coated with hot tar—and it is a blessing that such angels exist as those who staff the Oakland Animal Shelter and the Hopalong Animal Rescue (*www.hopalong.org*).

One of ten Dalmatian pups born in a single litter, Sophie was deaf, and suffered from a malformed jaw. Additionally, she possessed one blue eye and one brown eye. Because of Sophie's twisted jaw, dog breeder Robbie McHenry had to break up all Sophie's food in order for the puppy to be able to chew it. Other breeders advised Robbie to put the puppy out of its misery and put it to sleep, but she told them that she just couldn't bring herself to do it.

New owners quickly adopted the other pups in the litter, but Sophie remained in the kennel, unwanted and alone. Once again, Robbie's friends advised her to put the puppy down, but Robbie defended her soft heart by pointing out that Sophie had developed her own distinct personality. And, in spite of the pup's various infirmities and somewhat bizarre appearance, Robbie firmly believed Sophie deserved a chance to live.

Destiny may have dictated that it was the unwanted and rejected Sophie who was standing on the bank that chilly Sunday in March, 2003, when five-year-old Georgia Peck fell into the swift-moving river waters. Although she was only a six-month-old pup, Sophie appeared to draw upon her instincts and knew that she should swim to the struggling child and pull her to safety.

After Georgia had been rescued from the river at Corsock Mill, near Galloway, Scotland, she told reporters of Sophie's heroism. As soon as she had fallen in the water, Sophie had plunged in and swam over to her. Georgia said that she knew Sophie couldn't hear her screams, but she came anyway. Georgia grabbed onto Sophie's paw and held on fast until they had reached the riverbank. By that time, Georgia's mother, who had heard her screams, was standing there with others to help pull the five-year-old girl from the river.

Everyone agreed that Sophie was a remarkably strong swimmer to have been able to swim against the swift river waters with a child holding fast to one leg.

Robbie speculated that Sophie's strength as a swimmer may have been compensation for her other physical defects. The heroic puppy had proved once again that the potential for courage may lie in even the most unlikely of individuals—disabled or not.

tormy, an Anatolian shepherd puppy, became an important part of Marilyn and Skip Harned's family on Independence Day, 1994. The female pup was only ten weeks old when she entered the home of the Alpine, California, couple but she seemed full of life, love, and energy.

Two weeks later, Stormy was stricken with meningitis. Another more practical, less caring family would probably have put a newly acquired puppy with such a disease down without any further discussion beyond the veterinarian's diagnosis. The Harneds, however, stood firm in their resolve that they would not resign their little girl pup to such a brief existence. For forty-eight hours, Marilyn and Skip watched over Stormy while her little body hovered between life and death.

Stormy survived the crisis, but she was left paralyzed from her shoulders back.

Who could blame dog owners who would decide that it was no longer feasible or economically viable to continue to provide care for a twelve-week-old puppy that was paralyzed? Even the most soft-hearted of dog lovers might decide that it would be inhumane to keep a puppy alive that could not move its hindquarters.

But the Harneds never lost faith in Stormy. They saw in the puppy's eyes a fierce determination unlike any they had ever before witnessed in a dog. *This* was a pup that would not give up.

Incredibly, after several months of agonizing persistence, Stormy regained the use of her limbs.

Even more incredible, almost *too* impossible to believe, was the time when Stormy went on to become the first Anatolian shepherd Dog American Kennel Club Champion of Record.

Then, in 2000, while the Harneds and Stormy were participating in the filming of the American Kennel Club breed video, Skip suffered a debilitating stroke. Although he survived, the doctors informed him that he was in for a long period of ongoing rehabilitation.

Stormy seemed to accept Skip's impaired condition calmly, and she recognized that she had a debt to pay this man. It was as if the indomitable dog realized that it was payback time, and she was more than willing to stand by the man who had nurtured her back to health from the paralyzing meningitis. Stormy became Skip's constant companion, maintaining guard at the foot of Skip's hospital bed. Later, as his condition improved, Stormy never failed to accompany him on his therapy walks or to sit with her head on his lap as he worked at the computer.

Skip and Marilyn Harned had never failed to support Stormy during the times of her health problems, and now the caring Anatolian shepherd motivated her beloved owner to face his long-term therapy with a positive outlook. The loving manner in which Stormy devoted herself to Skip's rehabilitation inspired the Harneds to continue with the same resolve they had exercised when their little puppy conquered her illness.

*K*ermit the Frog bemoaned his color by telling us that it isn't an easy matter being green. But after all, Kermit is a frog. He's supposed to be green, and he had better come to terms with his biological status! But what about a Labrador puppy who was born green? Or a golden retriever who came out not so golden, but a lime color? Fortunately Montgomery, the Labrador pup who was born green just a few days before St. Patrick's Day, had loving owners with a sense of humor. And Wasabi, the dark green golden retriever, had an owner who admitted that he was mystified about the color of his pup, but who declared that there was nothing wrong with the little guy.

On Wednesday, March 9, 2005, Shannon Prosser of Saskatoon, Saskatchewan, was watching over her black Labrador Jenna as she delivered nine puppies. She was astonished when the fifth pup, a female, came into the world wearing a coat colored a bright shade of lime green. Shannon's first thought was that no one would believe her—they would think she had dyed the pup in preparation for the St. Patrick's Day festivities.

Shannon and her husband Tim had bred their black Labrador with a chocolate Labrador. This was their first attempt at breeding the two dogs, so they really didn't quite know what to expect. Shannon called a friend who bred chocolate Labs and asked her if the pups ever came out green. Her friend, surprised by the question, said that she had never seen a green dog and wondered if Shannon was teasing her.

The Prossers telephoned veterinarian Haider Elbermani, who ran the Prairieland Clinic. He had no explanation for them, but he did say that once before he had seen a green puppy and that the coloration had become normal when the dog matured. He assured the Prossers that the puppy's bright lime green coat shouldn't affect its health.

Ken Cockwill of the Western College of Veterinary Medicine admitted that he was baffled by the puppy, now named Montgomery after an Irish relative of the Prossers, but offered a theory that sometimes the fluid surrounding puppies in the mother dog's placenta can be green. Cockwill told Janet French of Saskatoon's *The Star Phoenix* that he wasn't certain that such greenish fluid in the amniotic sac could stain puppies, but he really couldn't offer another clue to explain the green Montgomery.

Shannon Prosser told Ms. French that she knew people suspected that she had gone too far and purposefully dyed the puppy for St. Patrick's Day. She added that if the little female stayed green, she would keep her. She didn't want breeders to buy Montgomery only to exploit her unusual color.

While there appears no real reason for Montgomery's lively green St. Patty's coat, there are occasional cases of a puppy's coat being an unusual color as the result of a discernible cause.

On November 14, 2005, a California dog breeder from Alhambra, was mystified to discover that one of the litter born to a golden retriever was colored a dark green. Local veterinarians told him that it was possible for a newborn pup's fur to be green because of the color of the placenta having rubbed off on its coat during the birthing process.

The vets declared the little retriever sound in body and brain, and its owner was unruffled by the pup's green hue. He decided to name the puppy Wasabi, after the spicy green Japanese mustard that people eat with sushi.

Puppy Miracles

hen Margaret was six-teen, she was involved in a serious accident in her hometown in the Midwest. It had been a hot day in August, and she and her friend Ruthie Johnson were riding their bicycles to get an ice-cream soda at the corner drugstore. Margaret's faithful beagle pup, Pudge, followed in close pursuit. None of them saw the car that roared past the stop sign. Later, witnesses would say that the driver seemed to be in an alcoholic daze as he accelerated directly toward the teenagers and the puppy.

All that Margaret remembered was something hitting her side, and then flying through the air. It seemed to take forever before she hit the sidewalk and rolled over on her back.

"I think I was knocked out for a while," she said, "and the next thing I remember was Ruthie kneeling beside me, crying, holding my hand. Faces of men and women bobbed up and down behind me, and I heard a lady say that she had called the police and an ambulance. I knew that I must be saying something, but my voice sounded so far away that I couldn't hear what I was saying."

Margaret's time in the emergency room is equally distorted in her memory. Although it felt to her as if she had broken every bone in her body and skinned every square inch of her flesh, she heard the doctor talking about a mild concussion and telling two nurses to clean up all the bloody scratches that had bits of sand and dirt in them. Margaret understood that she was to spend the next two nights in the hospital for observation.

"That's when I really began to remember what had happened to me and when I started to worry about Pudge, my eleven-month old puppy," Margaret said. "I had been staying with Ruthie and her folks because my parents were out of town for a few days."

Later, when she lay back against the pillows in her hospital bed, she began to cry. She knew that Ruthie's folks would call her parents, and they would be there as soon as possible, but Margaret really wished that they could be there right now. She really needed her mom's and dad's kind words of comfort.

And Pudge! How she wished that he were with her to lick her face and be with her in the room. The hospital corridors were echoing with strange sounds and the whole place smelled of antiseptics and medicines.

Pudge, so named because he had been such a plump little puppy, had slept on her bed every night since he was housebroken. The energetic beagle had been her faithful companion, never scolding her or contradicting her. He had listened to all of her complaints about boyfriends, teachers, and the "terribly unfair" rules of her parents. And when she told Pudge a secret, she could be certain that the beagle's lips were sealed.

During that night in the hospital, Margaret was awakened by something pushing up against her feet. She sat up as far as her throbbing head would permit, and was startled to see Pudge sleeping at her feet.

Her loyal friend had found someway to get into the hospital unnoticed. Margaret was overjoyed to see him, but also concerned about what would happen if any of the nurses discovered a dog in her room.

Pudge snuggled up to her face and licked her cheeks. "After I hugged him for a few minutes, I told him that he had better go home before someone caught him in the hospital," Margaret said. "Pudge whined and moved even closer to my chest. I remember wincing at the pain from my bruised ribs."

Just then a nurse entered her room with a flashlight, and Pudge jumped down and ran to a shadowy corner.

"I decided to explain in my best adult manner that my dog had missed me so much and had been so concerned for me that he had somehow managed to get into the hospital," Margaret said. "I asked her not to be angry, and perhaps, I suggested, some kind person might take Pudge home to the Johnsons."

The nurse moved the flashlight beam all around the room. She smiled and told Margaret that she had been dreaming. There was no dog in the room. She poured Margaret a fresh glass of water and said that she would return with something to help her sleep better.

"I concluded that tricky old Pudge had managed to beat it out of there without the nurse seeing him," Margaret said.

When her parents arrived the next morning, the first thing Margaret wanted after all their hugs and kisses were to know if Pudge had got home all right. She explained how the beagle had sneaked into the hospital in the middle of the night and had managed to escape being caught by any of the nurses on duty, so she hoped that he made it home safely.

"The look that passed between my parents hurt more than the concussion," Margaret said, concluding her story.

"Dad explained that they had received the emergency call from the Johnsons at around six o'clock had and arrived back home about 3:30 A.M. They had found a trail of blood that led to the back porch, one of Pudge's favorite hiding places. It was immediately apparent to them that the car had hit Pudge as well. In his pain and confusion, he had run back home.

"My parents sat with Pudge, trying their best to comfort him. He died around four o'clock that morning. Mom said that he gave a soft, little whimper, a long sigh, and then lay still. I will always cherish the memory of his final visit to me in the hospital—a visit that my dear, faithful Pudge made from doggy heaven just a half hour after his spirit left the earth."

*P*etre Preda, a Romanian shepherd, was checking his flock in the mountainous region of Magurii Casinului in Vrancea county when a bear charged out of the bushes.

Preda began to run for his life because he knew that the monster would kill him if it got its paws on him.

Preda ran as fast as he could, until he stumbled and broke his right leg. He thought that now only God could help him, and he began a prayer that he was certain would be his last.

That was when Preda heard the sharp barking of his little Pekinese pup. Preda moaned as it was apparent that both he and his beloved little dog would die at the claws and teeth of the bear. For the twelve-pound wee warrior to attack a huge bear would be suicide.

Preda's wife had given the Pekinese to him as a birthday gift, adding that the puppy would take care of him in the mountains. Preda had laughed at the image of such a tiny dog protecting a grown man, and he had named the Pekinese Bear, as a joke. But now there was no humor in the deadly confrontation and Bear squared off against the ferocious bear.

Amazingly, Bear's angry barking distracted the brute. The bear made a vicious swipe with his paw at the Pekinese, which would have surely torn him to pieces if it had connected with Bear's little body. Bear darted out of the path of the deadly claws and ran between the bear's legs to nip it on its stomach.

The bear roared in confusion and stood up on its hind legs, turning its head to look first at Preda, lying sprawled in pain with his broken leg, then at Bear, who took advantage of the beast's momentary distraction to bite it on the left leg.

That aggressive action on the part of the Pekinese appeared to make up the bear's mind as to which of the two victims it would attack first. The bear dropped once again to all fours and began to chase Bear.

Preda screamed in terror as he saw the little puppy running as fast as its legs could carry him. Bear ran into the woods with the large, shaggy giant close on his heels.

The shepherd feared that he had seen the last of his brave little Pekinese.

Petre Preda was only half conscious when a fellow shepherd discovered him lying a few feet from the flock of sheep that had begun to gather around their fallen master. After his friend had fashioned a crude splint for his broken leg, Preda told him of the bravery of little Bear, who had given his life to draw the bear away from him. In spite of his pain, Preda insisted on going into the woods in search of his courageous Pekinese's body.

Preda had just begun limping toward the forest, leaning on his friend's shoulder for support, when Bear came running out, completely unscathed, barking triumphantly. The little Pekinese had managed to outrun his much larger adversary.

Preda told the *National* newspaper that he thought that he was doomed when the bear suddenly charged him from the bushes. When he fell and broke his leg, he was certain that the brute would tear him to pieces. He would always be grateful that his little Pekinese had other ideas about how the encounter would end.

*D*oes dog saliva have the power to kill bacteria or even heal wounds? This question was considered in a 1990 study conducted at the University of California, Davis, which found that dog saliva killed *E. coli* and *Streptococcus canis*, two very harmful bacteria. In another study in Fairbanks, Alaska, in 1995, researchers collected saliva samples from 102 dogs and found that the spit inhibited the growth of certain bacteria, particularly nose mucous bacteria. The experiment concluded that while dog saliva may not be the next miracle drug, it did possess a number of unusual medicinal characteristics. Although such claims of wonder healings may be largely anecdotal, there are documented cases in which evidence is presented to prove that dog saliva has cured deadly insect bites, cancer, and blindness.

One person who has experienced this healing power is C. W. Martinez. In the spring of 1999, C. W. Martinez was walking with Villa, his ten-month-old German shepherd/Labrador mix, when he slipped on some wet rocks on a rugged nature trail outside of Santa Fe, New Mexico.

"It was very early in the morning," Martinez later told reporters. "I love to walk just after dawn when the world is beginning to come alive. I was carefully picking my way over these large, wet rocks when my concentration lapsed. I slipped, then fell to the ground."

The fall badly bruised ribs on his right side and gave him a slight concussion when his head struck the rocks.

"When I regained consciousness, Villa was licking my face, and my cheeks and forehead were wet with his saliva," he said. "If he had not brought me back to consciousness when he did, the doctors said that my concussion could have worsened, and one or two of my broken ribs might have punctured a lung. The longer I lay with my body weight against the large rocks, the more injuries I could have sustained."

It was then that Martinez realized a disadvantage to his early dawn walks. No one else was out enjoying the view of the sunrise in the countryside.

"Once I was conscious, Villa began barking very loudly," Martinez said. "I had no idea the pup could bark and howl so fiercely."

After about ten minutes, a young couple in sweatsuits and jogging shoes came to investigate the ruckus that Villa was causing. The woman had a cell phone with her, and she immediately called the police and summoned a paramedic team.

Villa had joined the Martinez family just six months before when they had rescued the four-month-old abandoned pup from an animal shelter, where the managers had given the scrawny German shepherd–Labrador only one more week before they would deliver him to the veterinarian to be put down.

"I guess Villa knew it was payback time," commented Mr. Martinez.

The paramedics ran into a problem when they first arrived to pick up the injured man lying on the rocks. Villa wouldn't let anyone touch his owner.

"I kept telling him that it was all right, that they had come to help me," Martinez explained. "Villa wasn't buying it. I think it was their uniforms that upset him. You know, the same unexplainable reason why some dogs hate postal employees with their uniforms and mail bags. Pretty soon, Villa relaxed."

Villa wasn't allowed to ride in the ambulance, but the jogger with the cell phone called Dorothea, Mr. Martinez's wife, and explained the situation. Because Dorothea is handicapped and could only drive to the start of the nature trail, the couple met her there with Villa.

Both the Martinezes agree that it was Villa's persistent licking of Mr. Martinez's face that brought him back into consciousness and the struggle for life.

*I*n the first five years of her marriage, Kathy told us, "Our family name should have been Heartbreak, rather than Hodges."

Cal and Kathy Hodges desperately wanted children, but in five years of marriage, they had lost three children during childbirth.

"After the loss of the first child, a little girl," Kathy explained, "we were really careful during the pregnancy. I pretty much took to my bed for the last three months. In spite of all our precautions, the next two children, a boy and a girl, died during childbirth."

During her bed rest during her fourth pregnancy, Cal brought home a little fox terrier pup to keep Kathy company. "Cal had taken on an extra job to help with all the medical expenses," Kathy explained, "so he brought me Vixen to cheer me up during all the lonely hours when he was at work."

When the Hodges' determination to have a family was realized with the birth of their fourth child, Gillian, in 2001, they praised God for His kindness and mercy.

Gillian was premature, but otherwise, she was healthy. "She was so precious to us," Kathy said. "We were overjoyed."

Six weeks after her birth, Gillian came down with what appeared to be a cold. Immediately, Cal and Katy rushed their baby to a doctor, who assured the new parents that they were just overreacting. "Doctor Colburn knew that we had lost three children at birth," Kathy said, "so he thought he understood why we were so anxious. He told us just to put a humidifier in Gillian's room."

That night, as Gillian napped in her nursery, Kathy kissed Cal goodbye when he left for his part-time job, and then she tried to relax with a magazine in the living room.

After a couple of hours of reading, Kathy was falling asleep in her easy chair when Vixen began troubling her. "We had had Vixen for about six months," Kathy said. "She was housebroken and generally good about asking to be let out to do her business. But this was different."

Kathy opened the door and told Vixen to run outside and to "go potty," adding that she should hurry up—it was cold outside.

Vixen stood in the doorway, refusing to go outside.

"All right, you spoiled brat," Kathy sighed, thinking that Vixen just wanted to play with her rubber bone toy.

But Vixen ignored all encouragements to play. She even refused to have Kathy scratch her tummy or ears.

"She kept jumping up on my lap, then jumped down again and pulling at my jeans with her sharp little teeth."

Kathy scolded the fox terrier, telling her that a good pair of jeans cost money.

"As if Vixen cared about such matters," Kathy laughed. "I concluded that Vixen was just bound and determined to be a nuisance, so I sat down again to read my magazine."

At this point, Kathy recalled, Vixen gave her the strangest look. "It was as if she was attempting telepathic contact and was saying, 'Dang it, girl, how dumb are you?' "

In the next few seconds, Vixen ran off to the nursery, her toenails clicking on the polished wooden floors.

"Hey," Kathy yelled after the fox terrier, "no running in the house. It's a good thing for you that Daddy didn't catch you doing that!"

Then Kathy heard Vixen through the baby monitor in the nursery. "Vixen let loose with the most eerie howling sound I could ever imagine," Kathy remembered.

Alarmed, she ran to Gillian's room where the frantic Vixen was standing up on her hind legs, her front legs resting on the baby's bed, emitting the awful howling.

"Gillian was blue and gasping for air," Kathy said. "I dialed 9-1-1, and an ambulance took us to the hospital. Gillian was resuscitated for respiratory failure and diagnosed with a viral infection. If it had not been for Vixen, Gillian would have been a crib death."

Vixen quickly rose to heroine status in the Hodges' household. "I wish, though, I wouldn't have named her Vixen," Kathy told us. "Vixen is actually the name for a female fox, but the word has developed connotations of a woman who is conniving and bad-tempered. I wish I would have named her Angel, because that's what she is."

everly Hale Watson, author of such books of inspirational verse as *Reflections of the Heart*, shared the following poignant story of the passing of her dog Toby and the remarkable return of his spirit in a puppy named Joey.

For twelve years, Beverly and her husband Paul had a black miniature poodle named Toby whom she nicknamed Shadow, because everywhere she went, he was always at her side.

"We had a bonding between us that was unexplainable," she said. "Toby was more than just a dog."

But one evening when she and Paul returned home a bit later than usual from work, Toby was not there to greet them at the door.

"We began at once to search for him; and when we found him, it was evident that something had happened to him because he didn't have the use of one side of his body—nor could he move his head. We suspected that either he had fallen down the stairs or suffered a stroke. We immediately rushed him to the veterinary hospital for diagnosis."

Almost four hours later, Beverly and her husband were told that their beloved Toby had numerous physical problems and a disintegrating spine. The vertebrae in his neck were jammed together, making it impossible for him to move his head.

"The doctor suggested that we take Toby home, and he gave us two choices. "One, Toby could be kept on painkillers for the rest of his life and placed in an area where there were no stairs. Two, we could have him put to sleep."

The doctor wanted them to think things over carefully before they made a decision.

Beverly carried Toby out to their car. "I sensed he knew that we needed to spend some time alone. When we arrived home, I began to receive very clear thought messages from him. He requested that I not lay him in his bed, but fix him a place where he could sleep on an angle so his

Puppy Miracles

head could lie evenly with his body. As I sat next to him, he communicated that he didn't want me to leave."

The next morning, Beverly and Paul decided that it was not fair to Toby that he should suffer, so they made the decision to return to the veterinarian to have their dear poodle put to sleep.

"Toby could move very little, so we carried him inside. As soon as we set him down on the floor in the examination room, it was as if he knew what was going to happen. All of a sudden he began walking briskly around in circles. He had a happy face, and his tail was wagging."

Beverly and her husband left the room knowing that Toby's pain would soon be over. She was also well aware that she would be lost for a while without her best friend.

"Walking to the car, Toby's spirit came through to me in thought messages once again. *He was free.* He communicated that he no longer had any pain, and he told me to envision him as a lamb leaping over the clouds. As I sat down in the car, trying to hold back my tears, Toby's thoughts continued to give me peace and comfort."

And then Beverly received a most extraordinary message from Toby's spirit:

"One day in the future, you will receive a telephone call from a woman moving out of the state. She will not be able to take her one-year-old silver-gray poodle puppy with her. She will request that you take him. When the call comes, you are to pick up the pup—*for I will be returning to you!*"

One morning in March, nearly seven months after Toby's death, Beverly was standing at her kitchen counter when the telephone rang to fulfill Toby's prediction.

"The woman on the other end identified herself and explained that she had been given my name by the Humane Society. She went on to say that she was in the process of moving out of state and due to housing restrictions in her new home, she would not be able to take her one-year-old silver-gray poodle with her. She could not understand her feelings, but somehow she just *knew* that I was to take her dog. She wasn't interested in selling him. He was a registered poodle, and her object was to find him a good home. Three people had told her that they wanted to take the dog, she said, but she knew that they were not to have him. Could I pick him up that evening?"

Beverly's first reaction was one of total disbelief. "I contacted my husband Paul and told him what had happened. We went that night to meet an 'old friend.'

"The owner greeted us with Joey tucked under her arm. As soon as we sat down on the sofa, she put him down on the floor and he went immediately to Paul. Joey jumped up on his lap and didn't move. After exchanging pleasantries and getting information about Joey's likes and dislikes, we departed with the poodle still clinging to Paul."

As soon as they arrived home and set Joey down in the foyer, he started checking out the house. Minutes later, he scurried up the stairs, heading for their bedroom.

"He leaped on our bed and quickly tunneled under the blankets to the foot of the bed. That is where Toby used to sleep. As we observed all of Joey's antics the rest of that evening, there was no doubt that Toby had indeed returned."

The next morning when Beverly and Paul opened the back door so Joey could have his morning run, they noticed something very unique about the way he ran. *He moved like a lamb, leaping over clouds!*

"It was an incredible sight to see," Beverly concluded her moving story. "Joey is proof that dogs *don't* die—their spirits live on."

*O*n a cold and frosty February night in 1985, the labor began. Bijou, the mother schnauzer, was huffing and puffing, giving birth to her litter of puppies. After twenty-four hours of work, the fruit of her labors appeared—four scrapping boys, one healthy girl, and one scrawny little girl pup who looked like she wasn't going to survive.

Thus began, said Jolen Marya Gedridge, the story of the dainty Gretchen.

"The runt was very dainty. She could fit in the palm of a hand, with room to spare. This little fur person was becoming a "failure to thrive" since she could not fight off the rough-and-tumble litter mates to nurse from her mother. So, we all had to make sure she got a few extra feedings alone with Bijou every day without the others. Within a few weeks, she began to plump to a nice size.

"The fun and pleasure of watching each personality develop in the pups was the best part. We could see who would be the leaders and who would be the lovers. Our little pup seemed to be almost invisible compared to the others. She was quiet and not much for playing; she preferred to cuddle on a lap or under a blanket. We figured she was going to be the quiet one of the bunch.

"When it was time to sell the pups, we decided to keep one boy and one girl. The scrawny girl won our hearts and she became our Gretchen.

"As Gretchen grew, we noticed she seemed to be not quite like the other dogs. After our veterinarian evaluated her, he said if there was such a term in the dog world, Gretchen would be diagnosed as mentally deficient. That never stopped us from loving her. In fact, she showed us many amazing and entertaining things she could do.

"One of the things we would roar in laughter over was her voice. She never learned to bark like a normal dog. Instead she would lift her head to the heavens and make a gurgling howl. We all referred to her as 'The Whiskey Tenor.'

"I learned what particular vocal sounds would set her off, and when I would come home from college, I'd always get her to rev up her 'gurgle maker' until the family had tears in their eyes. She didn't seem to mind that we laughed at her; she'd always wait for a pet or a treat for her gurgling antics.

"Although Gretchen was mentally on the slow side, she was an excellent hunter. She would dig a trench between two hosta plants in the backyard, then lay and wait for a tasty mourning dove to come bobbing by. Quick as a flash, she would dart out, grab the unsuspecting bird, and pop right back into the trench. Every spring day we would have to look for a pile or trail of baby bird feathers.

"Another special attribute of this pup was her walk. She actually had a definite bounce in her step, and even though she was only fifteen pounds, she could make the floorboards shake as she sashayed through the living room. We could feel the movement while sitting on the couch or the recliner. We often wondered how something so tiny could make a powerful step. She always had the pep in her step.

"Gretchen was definitely a gentle soul. Never offensive or aggressive—just a cuddler. She never begged for anything. And she never really could play like other dogs.

"I spent many hours with her trying to teach her a little game or find something that would interest her. We did develop our own special games of "I got your toe-toe," which I would gingerly grab one of her front button pads and give a tender squeeze. Then I would give her a little kiss on her forehead. She would then reach forward and lightly nibble my fingers. This was her way of playing and connecting with me. This was our special game and bonding activity.

"Gretchen had her favorite little hiding hole where she would sleep most of her days. It was in the corner of the living room, behind the couch next to the large antique trunk, which was under the bookshelf. She always had the need to be totally protected, and this hiding spot kept her out of the way from being stepped on. Every couple hours she would wake up from her doggie slumber, walk out from behind the couch, look at everyone, and then go back to her bed. As long as everything was status quo, she would return to her dreams.

"Perhaps most people would not think of Gretchen as a miracle dog or any kind of special dog, but to us she was. From her fragile beginning, she grew and developed into a grand old dame of fourteen years of age. Throughout her life, she was always 'puppyish' in her actions and thinking. A dainty puppy that never grew up, but had a rich and loving life nonetheless."

eslie K. of Chicago told of her strange experience about one evening as she was falling asleep, she heard the unmistakable growling of her old sheepdog, Chester.

Leslie was astonished to see the dog standing at her bedroom door, looking at something in the hallway that was obviously terrifying him. His teeth were bared and he was growling—a low rumbling, steady growl.

"Naturally, I was becoming pretty unsettled myself," Leslie admitted. "I was wondering just what in heck was in my hallway that was so frightening to Chester. I had had the duplex for about two years. It had been a friendly, quiet neighborhood. I hoped that night that it still was."

Reluctantly, Leslie went to investigate, carrying the baseball bat that her father insisted she keep handy under her bed clutched firmly in her right hand.

Leslie broke into nervous laughter when she saw that the only thing in the hallway was her little black-and-white rat terrier puppy, Duke who had been part of the scene for only a few months.

Chester was starting to get old, and his once keen expertise and talent as a watch dog had begun to lessen considerably. Her fiancé, who considered himself quite an authority on dog breeds, had told her that "you can't beat a little dog, like a rat terrier, for instance—Teddy Roosevelt's favorite breed—for barking and stirring up a fuss if someone tries to break into your place."

She scolded Chester for scaring the heck out of her. "What's wrong with you, you silly, old dog? Are you getting senile? And it is far too late at night to play some kind of weird dog game, pretending you're afraid of your buddy Duke. It's almost eleven o'clock. I have to get up extra early in the morning for a meeting. I don't need any weird little doggie games.

"And you, Mr. Duke," she said, raising her voice slightly in a tone of reprimand. "Just where were you at din-din tonight? You've learned to unlatch the doggy door, haven't you. Sneaking outside while Mommy was at work, not coming home on time for din-din, and then scaring poor old Chester half to death. If I wasn't so tired, you would be in for it, Mr. Duke!"

Leslie told us that she would remember forever the way that Duke just stood there, silently cocking his head from side to side.

"He almost looked as though his feelings had been hurt by Chester behaving that way toward him, growling at him and all. I had had Chester since I was a teenager living with my parents. I took him along when I got my first apartment after graduating from business school and now in the duplex. I had had Duke for only a few months, but the two animals had always got along together just fine."

The doorbell rang, and Leslie jumped, startled at the sudden sound. It was 11:10 P.M. Too late for company.

Cautiously, Leslie went to answer the door, hiding the bat behind her robe and whispering over her shoulder to Duke, "Don't take it personally, buddy. Chester is just being weird. But you are still going to catch it for getting out during the afternoon while I was at work."

Later, Leslie would wonder why she didn't notice that Duke wasn't barking at the ringing of the doorbell. Normally, he would be growling and barking up a fierce storm of protest at the very first vibration of the bell.

She unlocked the door when she saw it was her next-door neighbor, Josh. As Leslie opened the door, she was horrified to see that Josh carried the limp body of a small black-and-white terrier in his arms.

Puppy Miracles

"I'm so sorry, Leslie," he told her. "I just got home. I had to work late tonight. Before I left for work this afternoon, I saw Duke come out your doggy door and start to walk across the street to his favorite tree on the boulevard. This van came roaring down the street and hit him. Didn't even stop. I saw it all happen. Duke died right away, though. Thank God, he didn't suffer. I put his body in my garage. I didn't want you to come home and find him like that. I'm sorry I'm so late bringing him to you. I mean . . . what could I do? I didn't just want to leave you a note or something . . ."

Leslie could see that Josh had tears in his eyes. He was continuing to talk, pouring out a rush of regrets that seemed to blend into one single sound.

Leslie said that she had to struggle with reality for several moments before she could speak. It couldn't be Duke that Josh was holding. Duke was in the hallway where Chester was still staring at him as if he were seeing . . . a ghost!

She managed to mumble her thanks to Josh for his kindness and concern, then she took the crumpled, lifeless body of her little puppy in her arms and wept softly. It *was* Duke. His collar, his dog tag, his familiar rumpled fur. Josh once again softly repeated his regret, then said good night and let himself out.

Chester was still frozen in a posture of fear, but there was no longer any image of Duke in the hallway.

"When I gently lay Duke's body down in his doggy bed, Chester managed to break free from the rigid trauma that had held him fast—and he walked to Duke's body, lay his big head on the terrier's shoulder, and remained for the rest of the evening," Leslie said. "Duke's spirit had come to bid us goodbye, but he had nearly scared the life out of Chester in the process. Interestingly, Duke had presented me with the priceless gift of knowing that there is an after-life for dogs, as well as for people."

*S*cientists have declared the birth of a puppy named Snuppy one of the biggest stories of 2005. Of course, Snuppy is a very controversial, but very special pup. He is the first scientifically cloned dog. South Korean cloning pioneer Hwang Woo-Suk took some DNA from the skin cells of a three-year-old male Afghan hound's ears and replaced the nucleus of mature, unfertilized eggs from a female dog's fallopian tubes. A yellow Labrador retriever was the surrogate mother. After a normal pregnancy of sixty days, Snuppy was delivered by cesarean section on April 24, 2005. He was the exact duplicate of the adult Afghan from whose ears the scientists swabbed.

Snuppy is not the Korean version of Charles Schultz's famous Snoopy, the iconic beagle of the popular *Peanuts* comic strip, but stands for *Seoul National University Puppy*. Gerald Schatten of the University of Pittsburgh School of Medicine, one of Snuppy's cocreators, proudly pronounced the pup as normal, healthy, and frisky.

The research team had worked tirelessly seven days a week for three years, hoping to be the first to clone a dog. Scientists had previously cloned sheep, mice, cows, goats, pigs, rabbits, cats, a mule, a horse, three rats, and human embryos for stem cell research. Because dogs have such an unusual reproductive system, no laboratory had been able to clone a canine. The eggs of dogs are released from the ovary earlier than in other mammals, and all previous efforts to clone man's best friend had resulted in failures.

*S*angeeta was faced with a terrible choice when her husband screamed to save the children and to run to higher ground.

It was the morning of December 26, 2004, and R. Ramakrishnana, a fisherman from a village outside of Chinnakalapet, India, had just returned to shore, his boat filled with a successful catch. As he was walking home to his family, he heard a strange noise coming from the ocean, and he climbed to the rooftop of the two-story community center to investigate. He was horrified to see mammoth waves coming toward the village.

Sangeeta did not question her husband's orders to leave their hut immediately and to run to the top of the hill with their children. She knew that he was an experienced seaman who could quickly distinguish the ocean that supplied their food and their livelihood from an ocean that had suddenly turned dangerous, destructive, and deadly. Sangeet's terrible dilemma lay in the harsh reality that she had three sons, but only two arms with which to carry them to safety.

She picked up the two youngest, and shouted for seven-year-old Dinakaran to follow her. Faced with the prospect of outrunning the deadly tsunami crashing toward shore, the desperate mother felt that her oldest son had the greatest chance of gaining the safety of higher ground on his own.

But then she saw that the frightened and confused Dinakaran was not following her up the hill. He had made a deadly mistake in judgment. He had decided to seek refuge in the small family hut forty yards from the shore. Sangreeta shouted once again for Dinakaran to run up the hill. Then, as the waves were lapping at her feet, she turned away from him. With her younger sons in her arms, she exerted what little strength she had remaining to reach safety. With a great cry of anguish, she resigned herself to the thought that she would never again see her Dinakaran alive.

And it is quite likely that no one would ever again have seen Dinakaran alive if it hadn't been for their little scruffy yellow puppy, Selvakumar, who followed the boy into the hut. The pup possessed enough canine common sense to understand that a flimsy hut would offer no protection from the unimaginable power of a tsunami. Selvakumar grabbed the seven-year-old by the collar of his shirt and dragged him out of the hut. Once they were out in the open, the waves crashing around their legs, the pup kept nipping and nudging Dinakaran up the hill to safety.

Sangeeta had collapsed in grief as soon as she had crossed the main road at the top of the hill. Others from the village told her that they had seen the Ramakrishnan home collapse and carried away by the tremendous force of the waves. She knew that her husband was safe on the rooftop of the community center. She had her two younger sons clutched to her trembling sides, but Dinakaran was lost to her forever.

Her cries of sorrow were suddenly replaced with shouts of joy when she saw Dinakaran coming toward her, Selvakumar still steadfastly at his side.

While other villagers proclaimed the pup a hero and his rescue of Dinakaran a miracle, Sangeeta theorizes that her deceased brother-in-law was watching over his nephew that day, and saved Dinakaran from the deadly tsunami that would claim as many as 300,000 lives in Sumatra, Thailand, Sri Lanka, and India on that fateful Sunday morning of December 26, 2004.

*C*arla, an experienced emergency room nurse, told us of the near-tragedy that occurred to their cocker spaniel puppy, Rina, when the little female was just four-months old.

"My husband Ray and the kids were just coming in from the backyard to wash up for supper," Carla said. "Ray had been trying to do yard work, and six-year-old Nelson and four-year-old Niki had been helping him. I had watched them out the kitchen window from time to time while I was making the evening meal, and I had to laugh out loud. With the kids and Rina jumping around him, Ray had three times more work than if he were alone."

Carla heard the sounds of her family coming into the kitchen through the garage, followed by the mechanical moaning of the garage door being lowered.

"Then I heard a terrible yelp of pain and the kids screaming and crying," Carla said. "I ran to the kitchen door that led into the garage, and I saw that poor little Rina had got caught under the garage door when it was being shut."

Ray pushed the button again and the garage door was slowly being raised off the puppy, who was whining in awful pain.

Carla took one look at the crumpled Rina lying twitching spasmodically on the cement of the garage floor. The pup was trying desperately to get to her feet, but it was as if she had been literally broken in half.

"She must have gone back after her ball," Ray said above the cries of Nelson and Niki. "I thought she was clear of the door. I didn't mean to . . ."

Carla put a reassuring hand on her husband's arm. "It was an accident, honey. Of course you didn't mean to do it."

But it seemed the children weren't so certain. "Daddy shut the door on Rina!" they wailed nearly in unison. "Daddy hurt Rina. Now she's going to die, and it's Daddy's fault!"

Nelson, tears streaming down his cheeks, hugged Carla's legs and sobbed that Rina had to be taken to an animal hospital. "Mommy, you fix people in the hospital where you work. Take Rina to a place where they can fix her."

Carla knelt beside the injured pup and cautiously reached out to touch her.

"Watch out!" Ray warned. "Dogs go crazy with pain when they get hurt like that. She could bite you!"

Carla nodded in recognition of the warning, then carefully extended her fingers to stroke Rina gently on the neck.

"I think the poor dear was in too much pain even to notice me," Carla said, "but I slowly managed to feel Rina's broken little body. I could tell that as flexible as a pup's bones may be, Rina had suffered several broken ribs."

Rina whimpered pitifully, her tiny body trying to rebel against the pain and injury that held her fast. Carla winced when she made a preliminary evaluation that Rina's spine might also be broken.

"Please, Mommy," Niki had joined Nelson's plea, "take Rina to the doggy hospital!"

And then, with pointing fingers providing physical expression of their vocal accusations, Niki and Nelson shouted at Ray, "Daddy, you hurt Rina with the garage door. You have to take her to a doggy hospital! It's all your fault!"

Carla could see the emotions of confusion, anger, frustration, and helplessness moving across Ray's face. First of all, she knew that the children accusing him of deliberately smashing the garage door down on Rina was making him angry. He would never harm Rina—nor any other animal. Second, she knew that Ray was being consumed by an overwhelming sense of helplessness, because the family was going through a very rough financial stretch at that time. Ray knew that they couldn't afford to take Rina to a veterinary clinic for a checkup—to say nothing of what major surgery would cost. And third, Ray had guessed what Carla's professional medical experience had told her—Rina was beyond help from anyone.

Carla decided that it was up to her to tell the children that their beloved little cocker spaniel puppy had sustained a critical injury. And she also knew that even if there were a chance of saving Rina's life, it would take a miracle.

With the thought of mercifully and quickly ending Rina's suffering, Carla prayerfully considered how to tell Nelson and Niki the sad truth about their puppy. The sweet little furry bundle that was Rina, the bouncing ball of canine energy, the warm moist tongue that kissed them all with an expression of unconditional love, was dying. Although her words were carefully chosen, the children could not accept her sorrowful conclusion.

"No, no, no," Nelson firmly declared. "Rina is not going to die. God will heal her. We are going to pray for a miracle."

Ray spoke softly and placed a consoling hand on the top of his son's head. "It's too late for prayer," he told Nelson.

"I'm sorry that Rina got caught under the garage door, but life is filled with sad things that happen to people and to dogs and cats and everything on this planet. We just have to face the fact that Rina got hurt, she's in terrible pain, and we must be brave and let her go."

Nelson was adamant. "The preacher says that God answers prayers and that prayers can make miracles happen. I want us to pray for a miracle for Rina!"

Although they had a strong religious faith, Carla admitted that she and Ray joined hands with Nelson and Niki more as an act of bringing solace to the pain of their children over the loss of their puppy.

"But then something happened," Carla said. "I think as we formed that prayer circle around the crushed little body of Rina, we all felt a wonderful spirit of the Divine enter our hearts and souls. We all *really* prayed for a miracle healing."

And Carla said that whatever anyone thinks of her story, they received a miracle that evening at dusk as they prayed around the severely injured dog. After about fifteen minutes of intense prayer, Rina stood up and shook herself, as if she had merely stumbled and fallen while following the family inside the garage.

"That was twelve years ago," she said. "Rina got up and walked and came into the house to eat her dinner when we ate ours. I observed her carefully in the next few days, and Rina never even limped. In the years to come, she would deliver three litters of healthy pups."

Carla knows that some will believe the story of Rina's miracle healing and others will be skeptical.

"Remember," she concluded her inspirational account, "I am an emergency room nurse with over twenty years' experience. I am a thorough professional. I know that little Rina was crushed and had sustained broken ribs, suffered internal injuries, and may even have shattered her spine. But we all witnessed that puppy get up and walk, completely healed, after our family asked the Lord for a miracle. We received our blessing—a four-legged expression of unconditional love who is still with us today."

When Rex Miller, owner of the Greater Flint Prosthetic Center in Flint Township, Michigan, was fifteen years old, he lost his right leg trying to jump onto a moving train. As the wearer of a prosthesis himself and the creator of artificial limbs for humans, Rex was confident that he was the right person to fashion an artificial leg for Peg, a four-month-old puppy who was born without an ankle joint or right paw.

Peg's owner, Carol Beavnier, felt so sorry for her pup that she attempted to create a homemade artificial leg, using bandages and a plastic cone. The crude limbs never lasted for very long, especially with Peg, active as any puppy, playing tag and chasing her ball.

Researching her Peg's plight on the Internet, Carol found a Web site for handicapped pets and contacted Rex.

Veterinarians with Baker College placed little Peg under anesthesia and took X-rays to help Rex in his efforts to design an artificial leg for the pup. While Peg was under the anesthesia, Rex made a cast that would assist him in creating a new leg for the dog. The veterinarians at Baker College provided this service at no charge, because Peg's owner, Carol, worked for a nonprofit organization that trained puppies to become leader dogs for the blind. Peg, with her artificial leg, was going to be trained as a therapy dog who would visit elderly nursing home patients.

Rex admitted that forming an artificial leg for a puppy was extremely challenging. In order to prevent Peg from chewing on the leg, Rex made it out of material similar to bulletproof vests. He decided to attach the prosthesis with a harness made of a material similar to Velcro.

Rex acknowledged that a project of creating an artificial leg for a puppy would normally have cost the owner several thousands dollars. He was pleased with the results of his work on Peg, the future therapy dog. He said that Peg would always have "a little hitch in her giddyup," but she would do just fine.

anya Zirbel, a lifeguard trained in first aid, sprang into action when she heard the owner of a stricken Dalmatian calling for help.

"I was visiting from Wisconsin, staying with my cousin in a suburb of Los Angeles," Tanya said. "I was walking in the park, feeling the sun on my back, when I heard a lady crying out for help. At first I thought, *Oh, my. Welcome to L.A. Someone's purse just got grabbed or something.* When I looked around and saw the crying woman kneeling beside some bushes, I thought something must have happened to her child. When I ran over to help, I saw that she was crouching over a young Dalmatian."

According to Judith Lemon, her dog, Dante, had swallowed a rubber ball that he had found in the bushes along the footpath. She told Tanya that Dante wasn't quite a year old and he was still being trained to not eat everything he saw.

Tanya saw that the big pup's eyes had glazed over.

"I could see that he was in pretty bad shape," Tanya recalled. "His owner was crying and everyone in the group that had gathered around them were saying things like 'he's gone' and 'what a shame.'"

Tanya knelt beside Dante and dislodged the ball by pushing on his throat.

But the dog was still not breathing, Tanya knew mouth-to-mouth was the only option.

"I've done it many times," Tanya said, "but never on a dog."

Tanya heard members of the crowd gasp in disbelief when she placed her mouth over the Dalmatian's and performed mouth-to-mouth resuscitation. "I heard a couple of little kids making 'icccck' sounds, and one of them gagged, but I continued with my mission of saving a life," Tanya said.

After a number of breaths, Dante began to breathe, and Tanya further revived him with heart massage.

Owner Judith Lemon embraced Tanya and said that she couldn't thank her enough.

"Some elderly woman came up to me after the whole little impromptu drama and asked me how it really felt to give the kiss of life to a dog," Tanya recalled. "I told her that it wasn't too bad. Dante's doggy breath wasn't too bad, and there wasn't too much slobber because his throat was dry."

*W*henever Georgia walks along the river that runs through her small Washington community with her husband Ken and daughter Anita, their Chesapeake Bay retriever, Riley, is always nearby. Though he lost a leg from being struck by a motorist, Riley still gets excited about walks along the riverbank. Georgia will never forget the walk four years ago when Riley was just under a year old and was having just a bit of a problem with discipline, such as coming when they called him.

On this summer's day in late July, Riley ran off, completely ignoring both Georgia and Ken's calls.

"Dang him," Ken snorted angrily. "Look at him go. Like he's on an important assignment or mission and can't be bothered with listening to us."

In such a few more minutes, they learned that Riley really had a mission.

"What we couldn't know from our vantage point on the riverbank was that a thirteen-year-old boy and an eleven-year-old girl, tourists from Idaho, had been camping with their family and had gone swimming in the river," Georgia said. "The brother and sister found themselves caught in the river's current. The boy had reached the shore, but his sister had not. Riley had heard the girl's screams and had set out to rescue her."

Within a few more moments, the river's current had swept Riley and the girl into sight of Ken, Georgia, and Anita.

Georgia said that her jaw dropped open at the sight of their puppy's courage. "Ken yelled at him to get the girl and to be careful," she said. "Little Anita, only three years old then, just screamed and cried that her puppy and the little girl were going to get hurt."

Riley finally reached the girl, who managed to fight panic and according to Georgia, "listened to her angel, who told her to grab Riley's tail."

When he felt the girl had a firm gasp of his tail, Riley concentrated on fighting the powerful current and swimming toward shore.

"A couple of times the rushing water dunked both of them under, and I was afraid that Riley wouldn't be able to make it," Georgia said. "The boy had brought his parents from their camping spot to witness the desperate struggle in the river that would determine whether their daughter lived or died."

When Riley drew near the steep bank with the girl holding fast to his tail, Ken and the girl's father scrambled down amidst the rocks to wade into the water to complete the pup's dramatic rescue.

"It is fascinating how human nature works," Georgia commented. "The girl's mother didn't start shaking and crying until she held her in her arms. While Riley was bringing her daughter in to shore, the woman stood quiet and still, as if she were watching a story on television instead of in real life."

Everyone praised and fussed over Riley, treating him like the hero that he was.

"The girl's father gave Riley a whole steak that he had been grilling at their campsite," Georgia said. "Riley had the good manners not to refuse such a reward."

Georgia said that the family from Idaho took a lot of pictures of Riley, and the two families exchanged addresses.

"A couple weeks later, we got a sweet letter from the girl and some pictures of the wall in her bedroom," Georgia said. "She had a blowup of Riley pinned up next to some television and movie stars. She said that she had sent a picture of her heroes—and her special guardian angel."

Georgia said that from that day on, Riley had been her family's hero as well. She added, "But he's too darn frisky and mischievous to be our angel."

*O*n this particular January afternoon in 2000, the weather in southern Georgia was warm enough for three-year-old Winston Carter to play outside among the pecan trees in his grandmother Peg's backyard. At Winston's side was Arkansas, the Airedale pup that had been the little boy's constant companion since arriving eight months ago from Uncle Jake in Little Rock. Jo Ellen, Winston's mother, said that her son loved to crack and eat pecans, and so did Arkansas. As Jo Ellen sat inside the comfortable home chatting with her mother-in-law, she remembered hoping that both Winston and Arkansas were swallowing more nut meat than shells.

It was a very pleasant afternoon until Winston wandered over to a pile of loose hay that had been scattered over Grandma Peg's flower garden to protect the plot during the chilly months. Suddenly, Jo Ellen heard Winston scream.

"It was a piercing scream," Jo Ellen said later. "It was unbelievable. I had never heard Winston scream like that before. I don't know if I ever heard anyone scream like that before."

The two women stood up and looked out the big bay window to see what had so startled Winston.

"I just froze stiff as a statue," Jo Ellen said. "I said out loud, 'Dear Lord in Heaven, protect my little boy!'"

A three-foot poisonous black water moccasin snake, an unwelcome visitor to Grandma Peg's backyard from the swamp, had apparently been napping in the clumps of hay. When Winston's little tennis shoe had disturbed Old Mister Water Moccasin, it had struck at the boy's legs—and was now hanging by its deadly fangs from Winston's jeans.

Jo Ellen recalled that the snake seemed monstrous in size, thicker than her forearm. The big moccasin was jerking Winston with such violent movements that the boy's entire body was being tossed around.

Although the women seemed paralyzed with fear, unable to move, Arkansas immediately moved into action and attack mode. The Airedale, about thirty pounds at that time, leaped directly on the snake and grabbed it in his jaws. Next, the pup put his front paws on Winston's leg and kept shaking the snake back and forth until he got it free of the boy's jeans.

Although the left leg of Winston's jeans was sprayed with venom and bore two fang holes, the deadly moccasin had not bitten the three-year-old. As the doctor at a nearby clinic said after he had examined Winston, a bite certainly could have killed him.

That night for his dinner, Arkansas got a heaping dish of corned beef hash, his favorite meal after pecans, as a special reward for saving his young friend.

*V*alerie Locklear of Staunton, Virginia, really had no special expectations when it came to her black labradoodle, Oakley. To Valerie, the poodle-Labrador mix was a terrific friend, and she was satisfied to accept him as a somewhat ordinary, but loving, dog.

However, there is no debate that from the very beginning of their relationship, nine-month-old Oakley, Valerie's first dog, was kind of special—and kind of expensive. Because Valerie suffers from asthma, she had to get a dog that didn't shed. Research informed her that a first-generation mix of a poodle and a Labrador retriever, a *labradoodle*, does not shed. Oakley was cute as could be, but since labradoodles cost between $900 and $1,500, it took some careful budgeting to afford him on her salary as a special education teacher at Thomas McSwain Elementary.

On September 12, 2004, Valerie Locklear learned that Oakley had what it took to be a rescue dog, as well as a constant canine companion.

Oakley woke Valerie up with a series of uncustomary barks at seven o'clock on Sunday morning. According to his owner, who admitted to being completely puzzled by the outburst, Oakley never lets loose with such a barrage of steady barking.

A few moments before the outburst, Valerie had been aware that their elderly neighbor, who was in her nineties, was leaving her apartment. But, as she told Chris Lassiter, a reporter for the *News Leader*, Oakley knew her and never barked at her.

After a few minutes more of Oakley's peculiar behavior, Valerie began to become worried that an intruder had broken into her house.

Finally, in an effort to solve the mystery of Oakley's uncontrollable barking, Valerie followed him outside to investigate.

That was when she discovered that her elderly neighbor had fallen, and that a motorist had just stopped to help. Oakley had been trying to tell Valerie that their neighbor needed assistance—and needed it badly.

Immediately, Valerie summoned medical assistance. The ninety-plus-year-old woman was taken to Augusta Medical Center, where it was determined that she had broken her arm in the fall.

Later that same afternoon, the woman's son stopped by to personally thank Valerie for calling for medical help for his mother and to thank Oakley for raising such a determined commotion. Valerie admitted that the experience caused her to realize how smart Oakley really was. In fact, she has now enrolled him in puppy school. In addition to being "the sweetest, most caring dog," perhaps he can become the most educated.

"The average dog is a nicer person than the average person."
—Andy Rooney

Sometimes Andy Rooney can seem like a bit of an old curmudgeon on his regular Sunday night segment on CBS's *60 Minutes,* but few people will argue with his observation that some loutish humans perform and commit inhumane acts on their puppies. Another truism of canine-human interaction was noted by M. Acklam. "We give dogs time we can spare, space we can spare, and love we can spare. And in return, dogs give us their all. It's the best deal man has ever made."

The United Kingdom's *Eastern Daily Press* and *The Sun* newspapers reported the story of Lucky, a newborn terrier who was dumped in a shallow grave, covered up and left to die.

On July 28, 2002, passerby Keith Boore heard faint squeals emanating from the ground. He got down on his hands and knees and reached through the soft earth that had recently been pushed into the hole. After he had removed quite an amount of soil, he suddenly uncovered what he could only identify initially as defrosted chicken. But when he managed to get his hand under it, the "defrosted fowl" moved.

Boore brushed the earth from the thing's mouth and at last realized that the creature was a newborn terrier pup, and that it was still alive. Boore rushed the puppy to a veterinarian where the little terrier, named Lucky, received emergency life-saving treatment.

Later, Lucky was brought to Buttons veterinary surgery in Lowestoft, Suffolk, where veterinarian Sara Oldman managed to bring the terrier's nearly frozen body temperature closer to normal. The conscientious vet fed Lucky with a bottle and carefully monitored his recovery progress throughout the night. As he "defrosted," Dr. Oldman discovered that Lucky was very hungry. She fed him every two hours during the night, and by morning he was fine.

Inspectors from the Royal Society for the Prevention of Cruelty to Animals investigated the incident and issued a condemnation of the act, proclaiming it "unbelievably cruel."

For a wee pup resurrected from its grave, Lucky's good fortune continued when he was given to his newly adopted mother, a Jack Russell terrier.

Laddie, a German shepherd puppy, was only a few weeks old when he was hit by a car. At that time, his owners were members of a religious group that rejects medical treatment for its human members as well as for its animals, so the pup was forced to languish with a shattered leg.

When gangrene finally set in, Laddie's owners decided to end his misery by shooting him.

Laddie's present owner, Lorne Kerr of Elora, Ontario, said that the dog's guardian angel appeared in the form of a neighbor who halted his execution and took him to a veterinarian. The pup's leg had to be amputated, but Lorne thought there was nothing wrong with a three-legged dog, so the woman gave Laddie to him.

Five years later, in February of 1994, Lorne and Laddie, whom he had nicknamed Tripod, were enjoying a moonlight stroll when they happened upon a crew shooting a scene for *Trapped in Paradise*, a motion picture with Nicolas Cage, Jon Lovitz, and Dana Carvey.

Writer Bob Burns quotes director George Gallo recalling his first sighting of Lorne and Tripod, "I saw this silhouette of a man with a cap walking his three-legged dog in the snow. It was poetic. I thought, 'Wow! This guy really loves his dog. I've got to put the pup in the movie."

Although there were no scenes in the working script that required the appearance of a dog—four- or three-legged—Gallo ordered Laddie written into three scenes.

Lorne was amused—and a bit amazed by the whole dazzling series of events. Laddie's formal training consisted of sitting and shaking hands. But that first night of shooting, Laddie performed like a seasoned actor. In fact, he was so good that additional scenes were written for him. Lorne was the first to agree that his buddy Tripod deserved to be a star.

The temperature was hovering at 30 degrees below zero in the suburb of Lansing, Michigan on that February twilight in 1998. Joe Prohaska, sixty-four years old, a successful businessman and a well-known dog fancier, took his two canine companions—Lakota, a twelve-year-old rottweiler, and Cheyenne, a yellow Labrador, just under a year old—for their daily outing. It *was* really cold, Joe acknowledged when his wife Uta challenged the notion of a walk in such freezing weather, but he told her that he didn't want to deprive his dogs of the excitement of their usual late afternoon walk. They almost always scared a rabbit in the nearby woods and took off on a wild chase before they returned, panting, and emitting large clouds of steaming breath into the winter dusk.

After passing through the woods without sighting any rabbits, the three companions headed home across a frozen lake. Prohaska teased the dogs that it was even too cold out for the bunnies and suggested that they walk faster before they froze to death.

As the dogs bounded ahead, Prohaska felt the ice give way beneath his snow boots. "I was walking along at a good pace," he recalled, "when I went 'crack' right through the ice. It all happened so fast that I thought this could be the final curtain for Joe Prohaska."

Hearing his master's cries, Lakota raced over to assist Joe, only to crash through himself. Lakota was nearly thirteen years old and had been putting on a lot of extra weight. The last time Joe had weighed Lakota, the big dog had scaled in at 125 pounds.

As the two of them thrashed about, all Joe could think of was that he and his faithful companion would meet the same fate. "I thought that Lakota and I would grow unconscious, then sink below the surface of the lake," Joe recalled. "I had read that a person who enters freezing water without special survival gear will start to fall unconscious in under fifteen minutes. I had never read any statistics on dogs in freezing water, but I figured we both had about the same amount of time left on Earth."

Then Joe and Lakota looked from their thrashing in the freezing water to see the pup Cheyenne coming toward them.

Joe yelled at the Labrador to go home. Get help. "I shouted between chattering teeth for Cheyenne to go home and get Uta," Joe said. "Actually, I knew there wasn't time for the dog to run all the way home and return with help before Lakota and I froze to death. I just didn't want him to die with us."

Cheyenne dropped to his belly and began to crawl toward the hole in the ice. Joe could see that the pup had a plan. "He was digging in his claws for traction on the slick surface as he moved steadily toward us."

Joe assumed that Cheyenne would present his collar to him so that he might try to pull himself out of the hole in the ice. "Cheyenne was a pup," Joe said. "He weighed, at that time, about forty pounds. I weighed in at nearly 230. I loved him for trying to pull me out of the lake, but I figured he was not heavy enough to do the job."

When Cheyenne got close enough for Joe to grab his collar, Lakota seemed instinctively to know what to do. The big rottweiler used Joe's back as a ladder to hoist himself out of the icy water.

"As Lakota stood on firm ice, shaking the water from his fur, I felt a moment of awful fear and depression," Joe admitted. "I thought that Lakota had crawled up my back to save himself. I felt myself starting to give up. I really couldn't blame the dogs, I thought. The survival instinct is strong. I expected at any moment that Lakota and Cheyenne would turn away from me and head back to the house and the warm spot in front of the fireplace."

But what actually did occur next was far from Joe's fearful vision. Both dogs crouched down on their bellies and cautiously edged up to their owner.

"I had felt myself ebbing away," Joe said, "But now I saw clearly that my devoted dogs had a plan to save me."

As each dog offered his collar to Joe, he wrapped his numb fingers around the leather straps. Then the two dogs bent to the task of backing up, clawing the ice inch by inch, pulling Joe out of the hole in the ice. Backward and backward they clawed until their master was safe.

Joe said that the hundred yards or so back to the house was composed of unbelievable agony. When the three of them staggered through the front door, they headed for the downstairs bath, and Joe brought Lakota and Cheyenne in with him to share a steaming hot shower.

"My dogs had risked their lives to save me," Joe Prohaska said, tears glistening in his eyes. "They could have run ashore, like a lot of humans would have, figuring it was too late to save me. But they stayed put until they pulled me out to safety."

*O*n August 20, 2001, Nebraska farmer Randall Sitzmann was severely injured in a machinery accident that would have cost him his life, if not for the actions of his quick-thinking—and quick-running—dog, Hambone.

While operating a hay-mower, the fifty-eight-year-old farmer stepped off the machine to remove a thick clump of weeds that had become caught in the mower blades, and he suffered deep cuts to his right foot. Accompanied by only his one-year-old Border collie, Randall lay helpless and bleeding profusely. Summoning all of his mental and physical strength, Randall sat up, tore off a strip of his shirt, and tried to fashion a tourniquet from the cloth to stop the flow of blood. He could feel himself begin to ebb into unconsciousness.

It was at that point that Hambone ran off, and within a few minutes managed to return with Randall's wife Beth. According to Beth, she had been going for a recreational bicycle ride to the village about two miles away. She was just leaving their lane and moving on to the road when the fast-moving Hambone intercepted her by barking, yelping, and whining. It didn't take a canine interpreter for Beth to understand that Hambone was desperately trying to communicate to her that something was horribly wrong. Beth immediately worried that something had happened to Randall. She followed Hambone back to the farm, saw her severely injured husband, and telephoned rescuers on her cell phone as she tried her best to slow the bleeding. Within a few minutes, Randall was in shock from loss of blood, but Beth had managed to slow the bleeding considerably.

Paramedics arrived and transported the farmer to the hospital, where his condition was soon stabilized. Medical and police authorities stated that the Randall could have easily have bled to death if the fast-running Border collie hadn't left the scene of the accident and gone for help.

"The reason a dog has so many friends is that he wags his tail instead of his tongue."
—*Anonymous*

We once had a good friend who owned a little Boston terrier who would carry on conversations with our friend. True, Jiggs wasn't forming precisely *enunciated* words, but for every verbal question, comment, or greeting directed to the terrier, he would respond immediately with a vocalization of his own. Jiggs would frequently engage in dialogues with complete strangers and almost always with members of his family. Jiggs truly appeared to be imitating the patterns of human discourse and perhaps even mimicking the words as they may have sounded to him.

Through the years, we have had other friends whose dogs have sung along with their human families during group musical activities. Whenever this one elderly gentleman of acquaintance of ours sits down at the piano to "tickle the ivories," his little dachshund stands up on his hind legs, leans his forepaws against the piano bench, and contributes his impassioned howls to the musical presentation. Another of our friends, who loves to sing selections from her favorite operas around the house, never gets through an aria without her massive Great Dane joining her for a duet. According to each of our friends, their dogs began the practice of chiming in on the sing-alongs as puppies, and it seems singing is merely another method that intelligent, lively, loving dogs employ to create closer bonds with their humans.

Brad's father, despite his lack of vocal talent, sang "to soothe the savage beast" within the wild dog Queen when they were painstakingly taming her to adapt to human life on the farm. Brad has followed his father's practice of singing to each of his own dogs when they were puppies, thereby forming within the canine psyche a familiar "theme song" that will endure throughout the dog's life.

Queen's song, fashioned by Brad's father, was a take-off on "My Darling Clementine." Brad's beagle Reb had his own morning greeting song *and* a special theme song, "Reb, the Thunderer." Moses had a basic song, "Moses Is My Main Man," another for his walk, still another for bedtime, and so on. Sherry soon picked up the habit and Moses needed to hear only a few of the opening notes of each to respond with the appropriate behavior. We heartily recommend a song or two to facilitate the training of your puppy and to encourage a deeper bond of communication between you and your pet.

*J*acquelin Smith is an animal communicator. The term *dog whisperer* or *animal whisperer* has become so trite that we hesitate to use such a abused label to describe Jacquelin. The problem has been that *dog whisperer* has been too often carelessly applied to individuals who have exploited an alleged ability to communicate with animals. Such charlatans and scam artists have muddied the field for those dedicated to a better understanding of humans and their pets. Jacquelin not only deeply and genuinely love animals, but she has also been gifted with a psychic ability to "hear" or "pick up on" an animal's thoughts and feelings. She is the author of *Animal Communication—Our*

Sacred Connection, a book that is filled with stories about her experiences with various species. In her book and on her Web site, *www.jacquelinsmith.com*, Jacquelin gives detailed guidelines on how to communicate with your puppy or other animals.

We asked Jacquelin to provide a special story about communicating with a puppy for this book, and she generously complied with the following.

"Marie called me to find out how to help her new collie pup, Chester, listen to her when making basic requests such as sit, down, and come. Also, she wanted to learn how to communicate telepathically with him so that they both could build and experience a strong bond between them.

"When I telepathically asked Chester about why he wasn't responding to Marie's basic requests, he communicated, 'I'm still adjusting to being in my body and learning how to use it. I'm also learning about how humans communicate. Sometimes it is hard for me to be still and listen to my person. I get frustrated because her thoughts jump here and there, and then I get confused and scattered and don't know what she wants me to do.'

"I explained to Marie that animals see the pictures in our minds. They also pick up on whatever we are feeling. So, if a person's thoughts are jumping here and there, that is what the animal receives. An animal will typically act out or mirror back to us whatever we are putting out on some level.

"Animal communication is not supernatural, but a natural, intuitive way of communicating with animals which most humans have forgotten. It is a two-way street. We can send as well as receive thoughts, feelings, and images with animals. Being human, we receive images, words, thoughts, and feelings from the animals. It truly is a heart-to-heart language. We can ask a question or send an image to a puppy or any other animal.

"Marie was excited about beginning the journey of learning how to communicate with Chester. It was obvious that she loved Chester and wanted to create a strong, loving bond with him. Chester was ecstatic that his owner wanted to learn how to listen to his thoughts and feelings.

"I asked Marie to sit down, and I showed her how to relax her mind and body. This will allow Chester to become more relaxed and focused.

"I helped Marie practice creating a clear image of Chester sitting. After Marie felt like she was able to do this comfortably, I asked her to send a beam of light from her heart to the wall. Next, I asked her to send the image of Chester sitting on the beam of light until she could feel it touch the wall.

"Once Marie was ready to communicate telepathically with Chester, she went through the steps while verbally asking him to sit. Within a few seconds, Chester sat down and gazed into her eyes.

"Marie squealed as her eyes filled with tears. 'This is a miracle!' Chester had received her clear image along with her spoken word.

"Marie went through this process a few times while I was still at her house. Chester responded almost every time, which was terrific. Then I asked Marie to do the communication without the verbal request.

"After Marie tried this several times, Chester sat and looked up at her.

" 'Wow! This really works,' cried Marie.

"Chester did not sit every time, which was fine by Marie. The main purpose of communicating telepathically with our beloved puppies or other animals is to experience heart-to-heart conversations with love. Animals desire and love to be heard."

$\mathcal{J}$ean and Bill Schirf of Edwardsburg, Michigan, said their Shih Tzu, Geisha Girl, so longed to give birth that she had even experienced false labor on a number of occasions. The miracle of motherhood came to Geisha Girl, albeit in an untraditional way.

In November 2004, Jean found two abandoned kittens, no more than two weeks old, in the woods behind the Schirf's Indiana home. Geisha Girl was more than pleased to become the mother of the two kittens, a male and a female—Dilly and Dally. At once, she began to clean and mother them.

In about a week, Geisha Girl began lactating and providing milk for Dilly and Dally.

Veterinarian Dr. Michael Lampen of the Bergman Animal Hospital in Cassopolis told a reporter for the *South Bend Tribune* that it was not unusual for female dogs, even those that had never before been pregnant, to have a false pregnancy "and exhibit all the signs of being pregnant except for the fact of having puppies. [The female dogs] will come into milk and the whole bit."

Jean helped Geisha Girl with feeding time for Dilly and Dally by bottle-feeding the kittens with milk every four or five hours. All was harmonious in the Schrif household—except for their two adult cats, Demi Moore and Jasmine, who were jealous of Geisha Girl and her feline babies.

*W*henever Brad thinks of the kind of fierce, maternal love that can be exhibited by a female dog, he recalls a dramatic episode in his family's life with Queen, the wild dog who came to love them so.

Queen delivered four puppies when she was little more than a pup herself. Estrous cycles begin normally in dogs between the ages of eight and fifteen months. With an average pregnancy lasting nine weeks, Queen may not have been even a year old when she found herself caring for four demanding pups. The whole family fixed up a place for her in the cob house and gave her some old blankets to snuggle in with her babies.

It was Saturday night, which meant a trip to town and a chance to go to the movies. Brad and his sister June were reluctant to leave Queen alone. Their mother and father assured them that Queen had everything under control.

When the family returned home around eleven o'clock that night, they were startled to see Queen outside of the cob house, staggering as if from exhaustion.

"Whatever could make her leave her pups unattended?" Mom wanted to know.

"Maybe Queen isn't such a good mother," Brad suggested.

"Wait! Look!" Dad shouted. He had left on the car's headlights, and they were suddenly able to see another figure in the shadows.

In a blur of motion, something came running at Queen and knocked her sprawling.

Queen rolled back to her feet, emitting a pitiful whine. She grabbed at something dark and furry with her teeth, gave it a shake, and tossed it five or six feet away from her.

Whatever it was landed with a thud, and Queen braced herself for another onslaught.

"My gosh!" Dad said. "It's a big muskrat!"

As the creature moved in the shadows, it appeared to be gigantic in size— the vicious king of all muskrats.

"It's after her pups!" Mom said.

They could see now that there were splotches of blood on Queen's white coat where the muskrat had bitten her. The huge rodent had smelled the newborn puppies and the afterbirth, and had come up from the creek to have a snack.

"Poor Queen," June said. She had fallen asleep in the backseat on the drive home from town and had awakened to the nightmarish scene. "We have to help her! The big rat wants to eat her babies!"

Dad was already on his way into the house to get the shotgun from the front porch.

Queen blocked another charge by the muskrat and yelped as the rat's prominent front teeth tore at her flesh.

With an angry growl, Queen got her teeth behind the creature's neck, shook it violently several times, and threw it as far away from her as her fading strength would allow.

The muskrat landed once again with a heavy thud, but quickly got back on its feet. It was tough, mean, and determined to feast on the puppies.

Queen's entire body was trembling with fatigue as she braced herself for another charge.

Just then, the roar of the shotgun blasted the unwelcome invader into bits.

Queen's ordeal was over. She collapsed, whimpering, her legs folding beneath her. Then, she struggled back to her feet and limped into the cob house to check on her babies.

Dad turned on the light in the shed. "They're all present and accounted for," he told us. "The muskrat didn't get any of Queen's pups."

From the looks of the grass in the yard, the deadly struggle between the new mother and the predator must have gone on for a long time. Once and for all, Queen proved that she had courage and heart—and that she was the best of mothers.

*S*hannon Neale told us that she spent a summer as a fire spotter atop a twenty-five-foot tower in dense Oregon forest country. Not surprisingly, she said that it was pretty rough living, and it got lonely. Her only companions were Bogart, her one-year-old German shepherd pup—and a ghost.

Shannon admitted that she was a bit of a control freak and an almost obsessive planner. "This was back in the 1970s," she explained. "I would be graduating from college as a forestry technician, so I wanted some practical field experience as a fire spotter. I would be twenty-two that summer, so I thought the sooner the better. I knew that living atop that tower seven days a week for the entire summer would get lonely, so in December I got a German shepherd puppy to keep me company. I figured that by the time we left for the forest tower in early June we would have bonded and that he would be big enough to be a good watchdog."

Naming the dog after Humphrey Bogart, one of her father's favorite tough-guy actors, Shannon figures that Bogart carried an image of a rough and ready, yet sensitive, guy. Those were the attributes that she wanted Bogart to develop as her buddy and sole companion for the summer.

Shannon's living quarters were a fourteen-by-fourteen-foot cabin perched on top of the tower. "Remember, this was back in the seventies, and the conditions were a lot rougher than today with all the modern technology," she reminded us.

Shannon had no electricity and no running water, but she got by with a bed, a stove, a cupboard, a hand-crank phone, and a transmitter radio. She had to pump her water supply from a fire pumper.

"I learned to recycle the water about a half-dozen times," Shannon recalled "First, I would heat it to make it safe for Bogart and me to drink. Next, I would wash my hair, take a bath, then use the water to wash out the cupboard and clean the floor."

Shannon's watch covered a twelve-mile radius. If she spotted a fire, her job was to line up its location on the fire-finder and do her best to pin it down within forty acres.

Then she called the ranger station so that someone there could notify the firefighters.

Shannon's first encounter with the ghost occurred late one night shortly after she had gone to bed. "I had been there long enough to be able to identify all the normal, regular night noises. What I heard that night clearly sounded like footsteps coming up the stairs to my cabin at the top of the tower. Bogart started to growl, so I know that he heard the sounds, too."

Shannon got out of bed to investigate. She knew there shouldn't be any rangers in the area that time of night, so whoever was coming up those stairs had absolutely no business doing so. Besides, the rangers would have called her first so they wouldn't scare her.

When she peered cautiously down the stairs, with a flashlight in one hand and baseball bat in the other, Shannon saw no one. Bogart was still growling, but the stairs appeared empty. It took her quite a while to fall asleep that night, because she kept expecting to hear those footsteps again.

"Thank goodness, I had Bogart with me," she said. "He helped me keep my courage up. And he was big enough and could look mean enough to frighten off any human intruder."

The mysterious sound of footsteps became a regular feature of nightlife in the forest tower. Never were the footsteps heard in the daylight, but they returned night after night to haunt the shadows of the tower steps.

"I heard those sounds a lot, and so did Bogart," Shannon said. "They actually became quite unnerving, and they kept me awake a lot of nights. I would lie there trying to figure out what could be making those kinds of sounds. Raccoons, opossums, weasels, coyotes, foxes? I tried to make up believable scenarios that would fit one or more of these nocturnal critters coming around after dark to try to snitch some food from the tower, but I couldn't make the 'ghost sounds' fit the kinds of sounds that I knew these animals would make.

"There were no bipedal animals in the Oregon woods—except for those stories about Bigfoot, Sasquatch, or whatever they called that giant hominid creature. But I figured something as huge as Bigfoot was supposed to be would make a lot more noise if it tried to come up the tower stairs."

Whatever was visiting Shannon and Bogart late at night, it was robbing them of their sleep time.

"As it was," Shannon said, "sleep was not all that easy to come by. I really envied Bogart when he would stretch out and take a couple naps during the day. I was expected to provide weather and temperature checks as well as keeping a sharp eye out for fires. Every day, around two o'clock in the afternoon, I had to take the wind direction and speed, describe any cumulus clouds in the area, check the humidity, and indicate how much the temperature had risen or fallen. If there was a lightning storm, I might be up all night, checking for any hits that produced fires."

A lot of Shannon's friends had asked her before she left for the forest tower if she wouldn't be afraid being out there alone in the woods all summer. "You know, Shannon, there are lions and tigers and bears lurking in the deep, dark forest," they would warn her, sometimes with mock terror—sometimes genuinely serious and concerned about her welfare.

Shannon would acknowledge that there were bears and mountain lions in the Oregon forests, but no tigers had been reported in the region since most of them had moved to India. Then she would put her arms around Bogart and give him a big squeeze and assure all those concerned that he would protect her.

But Shannon admitted, when she was recounting the story, that she would feel a shudder and a chill whenever they hear the ghost at night. "I never got used to the sounds of those footsteps coming up the stairs," she said. "And neither did Bogart. He would go nuts with growling at our invisible guest, and sometimes he would bark."

Once when she was on the phone with a ranger at the station, she admitted that she was hearing weird noises, like someone coming up the stairs at night.

"Oh no, not you too!" he responded with a wry chuckle.

Shannon wanted to know what he meant, if anyone else had heard similar sounds at night in the tower.

"It's nothing," the ranger tried to dismiss her concern. "Seems like everyone who takes that tower has reported those same weird noises."

Puppy Miracles

"So what causes them?"

"A ghost, I guess."

That was *not* the answer that Shannon wanted to hear. "That's not funny, ranger," she scolded him. "Do you want to come up here every night and babysit me?"

The ranger chuckled, declining the assignment. "It's too hot this time of year. Last time I was up in that tower in the summer, it felt like it was over one hundred degrees."

"And that's on a cool day," Shannon agreed. "So tell me about the ghost. Were you serious?"

The ranger paused. "Oh, I don't know. Some of us guys have just called it the ghost of old Trapper Joe."

Shannon wasn't going to let the ranger off the hook with such a brief explanation. She wanted to know who Trapper Joe was—or who he used to be.

"Well," the ranger continued, "there used to be an old trapper who lived by himself in that area. I don't know what his real name was, but he came to be like some kind of symbol of nature in the area. You know, like that Indian in those television ads who cries when he sees what a mess us white guys have made of the environment.

"Anyway, this old fellow always used to be seen by everybody picking up trash and helping to keep things nice and natural-looking. One day, someone noticed that we hadn't seen the elderly gent for a while, so we figured he must have died. And it wasn't long after that that the spotter who was in your tower started complaining about

Puppy Miracles   177

strange night noises. We told him that the ghost of the old trapper was just helping him do his job, looking out for forest fires and such."

The ranger's explanation of the eerie sounds was all Shannon needed to hear.

"After that, Bogart and I would just call out to the noises and wish them a good night. Whatever—or *whoever*—was causing those spooky sounds—it made me feel a whole lot better to give some kind of benign identity to them," Shannon said, concluding her story. "And doing so sure helped Bogart and me get through the long, hot summer in that tower."

*T*he first time that Jeremy Majorowicz spotted the gray and white husky pup sitting on the railroad bridge in the flats area of Chippewa Falls, Wisconsin, on the morning of December 23, 2005, he didn't think too much about the dog's strange perch—except to note that it was a darn cold morning for any human or canine to be sitting still in any one place for too long.

Majorowicz, a construction worker from the Minneapolis–St. Paul area, was working on the Comforts of Home addition in Chippewa Falls. The temperature that morning was below zero, and the wind chill factor made construction difficult. When the boss had said it was too cold to work, Majorowicz headed to a restaurant in Eau Claire for some breakfast before going back to his room.

About an hour and a half later, when he returned to the construction site to pick up his tools, Majorowicz noticed that the pup was still sitting on the tracks of the railroad bridge. Now he was getting really intrigued as to why a husky, a breed of dog that he knew loved to run, was just riveted to one spot—and on the railroad tracks at that. If the dog was told to wait in a certain place at his owner's command, the railroad tracks were a strange place to choose for a rendezvous spot. After all, there were trains using the tracks on that railroad bridge.

Majorowicz loaded his tools and began to head toward Pumphouse Road hill at Amstar Drive. That was when he saw that the pup was still there, sitting on the tracks.

Enough was enough. Majorowicz said later that he couldn't take it any longer. He had to solve the mystery of a healthy young pup who wouldn't budge from one particular spot on the railroad tracks.

When Majorowicz approached the dog, he could see that the pup had gotten wet and that he was shivering violently.

The construction worker, who himself has two dogs, could see that the husky was frightened. He offered the pup part of a muffin that he had taken from the restaurant, but the dog cowered back from his hand and wouldn't even nibble on the crumbs.

Majorowicz called the police on his cell phone, attempting as best he could to describe the unusual situation. When Chippewa Falls Officer Tim Strand arrived on the scene, he found what the construction had told him would be there—a nearly frozen dog, shivering "unmercifully," who refused to budge from the railroad tracks.

Officer Strand tried to call the dog to come to him, and then he reached out his hand in an attempt to grab the pup, but to no avail. He knew that the rescuers were working on a rather severe timetable. It was not long before a train was due on those tracks.

The police officer put in a call to animal control officer Al Hyde, who, upon arrival, hooked a noose around the husky's neck and attempted to pull him free of the tracks. The husky didn't budge.

That was when the men discovered the extent of their icy dilemma. The pup was literally frozen to the tracks. Officer Strand lifted the husky's tail and hind quarters, and the men could then see that its front legs and body were frozen to the metal track.

At that point there was nothing to do but give the pup a mighty tug. The dog gave forth a loud yelp and left quite a bit of hair on the track, but he was finally freed from the icy grip that had held him for many hours.

Ten minutes after the pup was freed, a train rumbled over the tracks where the dog, affectionately nicknamed Ice Train, had been held prisoner.

Thanks to construction worker Jeremy Majorowicz's feelings that something just wasn't right, that a husky pup wouldn't normally be sitting still for hours in one spot—especially when the temperature was below zero—and Officers' Strand and Heyde's prompt response to the unusual situation, Ice Train was saved.

Ice Train was brought to the Chippewa County Humane Association with icicles on his belly and very tender paws, but Vickie O'Branovich and her staff wrapped the pup in warm blankets and brought his temperature up to normal and his anxiety and fear down to zero. Ice Train was determined to have no lasting ill effects from his ordeal.

If construction worker Jeremy Majorowicz had not wondered why a darn fool husky pup chose to sit immobile for hours on a railroad bridge on a freezing cold December morning, Ice Train would surely never have run again.

*J*onathan Cooksley and his wife Nicola had never before owned a dog, but they fell in love with a starving puppy who followed them for eight hours as they hiked across a dormant volcano in San Miguel in the Azores.

At first they were amused by the manner in which the little fellow approached them and begged for a bit of Jonathan's sandwich for lunch. The Cooksleys could tell by the way the pooch gobbled the food and by the stark way his little ribs stood out that the pup was very undernourished.

Their amusement turned to astonishment when the puppy followed them up a mountainside, through thick undergrowth, across a volcanic lake, and eventually back to their hotel—a total of eight hours on trek.

A member of their tourist group identified the pup as a Portuguese pointer and laughed with the Cooksleys when they said that they had gained a companion while they were on holiday in the Azores.

A few days later, when it was time to return to their home in Dorset, UK, the Cooksleys planned to turn their new friend, whom they had named Mears after survival expert Ray Mears, over to an animal pound on the island. When Nicola inquired about Mears's future, the Cooksleys were told rather bluntly that the puppy would be put down almost immediately—but in a most humane manner.

That was when Jonathan and Nicola decided to acquire their first dog. They made the difficult decision to fly Mears home with them to Dorset.

By the time that Mears's period of quarantine (a standard requirement of pets arriving from another country) had ended, the Cooksleys had spent more than $8,000.

Nicola remarked that only one person had told them that she and Jonathan were crazy. Everyone else had remarked that the love story between Mears and the Cooksleys was "quite lovely." And, for Mears, a miracle.

*M*ichael Bosch, a sixty-three-year-old real estate broker from Nicasio, California, had been in touch with the Marin Humane Society for more than a year about adopting a dog. Unfortunately, in August of 2005 he suffered a heart attack and put off acquiring a pet for a bit longer.

Two months later, Michael contacted the Marin Humane Society once again and thought that he might adopt a Labrador that had been rescued from Hurricane Katrina. Once he was at the kennels, however, a "gangly-legged, floppy-eared," five-month-old cocker spaniel pup caught Michael's eye. A Labrador was very nice, but there was something about the little cocker spaniel. Without any more deliberation, Michael decided to take her home with him. It turned out to be the most fortunate decision that Michael ever made.

Bosch named the cocker spaniel Honey, and everyone could see that the two bonded immediately. In late October, Michael and Honey were heading out in the SUV, when the early morning sunlight blinded Michael and caused him to misjudge the turning range of his vehicle between the edge of his driveway and the deep ravine on the other side of the road. The SUV, with Bosch and Honey inside, rolled over five times, and landed upside down.

Michael, still recovering from his heart attack two months previous, was hanging upside down; his legs crushed and pinned down by a tree that had ripped through the roof of the car. He tried to fight, despite realizing that help probably wouldn't come in time to do him any good.

As his consciousness cleared, Michael assessed the situation objectively. They had fallen fifty feet down a ravine that was on an isolated seventy acres. The nearest neighbor was a quarter of a mile away. He was trapped, with no help in sight.

Michael looked down at Honey, whose brown eyes were desperately searching his own for comfort and reassurance. She was barely five months old. She was not Lassie or some fictional canine hero who could tell people that Timmy had fallen in the well.

But she was their only hope.

Somehow, Michael managed to push Honey through a hole in the windshield. "Go get help!" he told her. What else could he say?

Bosch had only owned Honey for two weeks. How much allegiance could she possibly feel that she owed him? They were strangers, really. She would probably just wander away and look after herself. What else could he realistically expect of a puppy?

Honey, however, was one of those dogs born to be a hero.

First, she had to make her way from the site of the accident through half a mile of thick bramble and a thick forest. After she managed to crawl up the ravine, she ran a quarter of a mile to the home of Robin Allen.

Robin later told authorities that little Honey pawed and whimpered at her door until she opened it. Then the cocker spaniel's manner and movements made Robin understand that she wanted her to follow. Robin stated that she knew the puppy was directing her, literally bringing her to the scene of the accident.

By the time rescue crews arrived, Michael had been hanging upside down for nearly eight hours. His pulse was weak, and if it had not been for Honey's summoning assistance, he would clearly not have survived.

Firefighters had to use the "Jaws of Life" just to get to Michael. He was airlifted to Santa Rosa Memorial

Puppy Miracles

Hospital to be treated for five broken ribs and leg injuries. He was later transferred to Kaiser Permanente Medical Center in San Rafael.

On January 10, 2006, the National Dog Day Foundation named Honey its Rescue Dog of the Year for 2005. Colleen Paige, a nationally renowned dog trainer and behaviorist, founded The National Dog Day Foundation.

"Honey was a dog that had just found a new family, but her loyalty was strong enough to save the life of her owner," said Ms Paige. "Honey is the perfect example of everything that dogs are capable of . . . of everything they contribute to our society."

Michael said that he was so honored to have his puppy Honey recognized in this way. "She deserves it," he said. "She saved my life."

The day of recognition was August 26, 2006 and was celebrated by a parade in New York City. The Grand Marshall for the parade was none other than Jon Provost, "Timmy" from the beloved *Lassie* television series. Honey had her very own float for the parade.

avid Van Slyke of Ohio told us that he received a six-week-old miniature "party poodle" on his nineteenth birthday. Party poodles, he explained, have two or more colors, a coat that is frowned upon by the AKC. Dave's poodle was black and white, and he named her Holly.

"It was a bitter cold January day," Dave recalled. "Holly was standing on the outdoor patio on the back of the house. Someone had just let her out the glass sliding door. Unknown to Holly, I was in the front yard wearing a heavy winter coat and a stocking cap that included a face mask. I walked around the corner and she saw me.

"Sensing that she had just come face to face with a monster, she let out a scream, bounded up the steps, and frantically barked to get in the house. I did not intentionally frighten her, and I felt badly about it.

"However, it had a good result. We lived on a four-lane highway. From that day on, Holly would *never* go into the front yard—because that's where the monsters lived. The mask had taught Holly the boundaries of her own backyard. She could stay outside all afternoon on a summer day, unattended, and never leave her backyard."

*B*ob Reuscher didn't need any assistance when he decided to costume his basset hound to look like some hideous creature straight out of a vintage Universal Pictures monster movie. Bob was quite capable of creating a four-legged nightmare on his own.

Bob told us that he loved Halloween ever since he was a boy of five and had first dressed up to go trick-or-treating, and he had worked steadily at becoming a connoisseur of all things spooky, macabre, and eerie. When he became an adult and had a wife and family of his own, Bob was still a fan of ghosts, ghouls, and other creatures of the night. When Halloween came, he tried to outdo the prank that he had pulled the previous year, and also create a more fiendishly frightening costume than he had ever before worn before.

Bob felt a fine sense of accomplishment on the Halloween when he had attired himself as the Scarecrow in the *Wizard of Oz* and had lain, as floppy and gangly as possible, in a lawn chair just to the side of the front door. As the little "munchkins" approached the Reuscher residence to ring the bell and shout their "trick or treat" warning, Bob would lie as still as possible. Just as the first little forefinger was about to press the doorbell, Bob would emit his most bloodcurdling scream and the scarecrow would come to life, waving its raggedly arms and stomping its boots at the kids.

At the same time, Bob's children, Monica, seven, and Mickey, nine, came running out from their hiding place behind the bushes dressed in their flying monkey costumes, shouting that they were going to carry the trick or treaters away to the castle of the Wicked Witch. While Bob admitted that he took almost fiendish delight in the ensuing screams from the little trick or treaters, he always rewarded them with generous handfuls of candy as compensation for sending some of them into near-traumatic states. Never mind the fact that some found it necessary to go home to change their Halloween costumes.

When Monica and Mickey were in grade school and off trick-or-treating on their own, Bob hid a speaker in the bushes midway up the sidewalk leading to their front door. Speaking in an eerie, croaking voice, Bob informed the wee trick or treaters that he was an invisible monster that craved either their candy or their little bodies for his dinner. After the initial jolt of being assailed by an unseen, cackling entity, the older children, well-versed in the ways of modern technology, laughed and challenged the disembodied voice to try and get their bags of sweet Halloween loot. At this point, Bob's wife, Steffi, would come out with candy bars to reward the brave resisters.

However, a couple of the very young kids were so badly frightened that they threw their treat bags at the invisible monster and ran screaming all the way home before collecting their reward. The following morning, Bob was advised by a couple of his neighbors that they had to sit up half the night with their frightened sons or daughters, assuring them that the invisible fiend had not followed them home and was waiting in the closet to snack on their toes. They suggested that in the future Bob should tone down his Halloween pranks.

In 2004, when both Monica and Mickey were away at college, Bob talked Steffi into getting a puppy to help combat the empty nest syndrome. Steffi mildly protested, reminding her husband about the collie that they had acquired when the kids were younger. Unfortunately, Bruce, named for Bruce Lee, the martial artist, had the temperament of a kung fu master on amphetamines—and after he had bitten each member of the Reuscher household at least twice, Bruce was put down.

Bob persisted in his desire to get another dog; Steffi relented, and they brought home a basset hound. Bob named him Boris, after the great actor Boris Karloff, the original enactor of the Frankenstein monster.

That Halloween, Boris was about eleven months old, and Bob decided that his puppy should be transformed into a monster. Steffi marveled at the hound's patience as Bob placed horns on the top of his head, positioned a hideous demon mask over his face, and covered his torso with greenish-colored hair.

In addition to his grotesque appearance, Bob was counting on a personal idiosyncrasy of Boris the basset hound. Ever since he was a couple of months old and he was let out the front door to do his business outside, Boris would charge out of the house and emit a fierce growl.

Bob and Steffi had always laughed at this peculiar habit of their hound. At first, they looked to see if anyone or anything was out in the yard. When there was never any man nor beast in sight, they theorized that Boris simply growled as a precautionary measure. That Halloween night, Bob would put that puppy eccentricity to good use.

"What if Boris should bite one of the children?" Steffi began to worry.

Bob quieted her alarm. "Boris is so gentle. There is no danger of his biting any of the kids. He'll just give them a good scare. Especially kids from out of the neighborhood who don't know we have a dog."

Bob didn't have long to wait to try out his secret spook attack. A group of six or seven trick or treaters with the requisite number of witches, vampires, and fairy princesses among them, approached the Reuscher residence. Just before any of them could ring the bell, Bob threw open the door, expecting Boris to charge out, growling and roaring at the usual suspects somewhere in the night.

But Boris froze in his tracks at the sight of the bizarrely costumed creatures of the night. It was as if the basset hound brain was telling Bob that he had been right all along. There really were unimaginable terrors out in the yard, just waiting for him to come out and do his business so they could grab him. He let out a long, mournful howl of terror and cowered behind Bob's legs.

The children crowded into the doorway, laughing at the dog with the horns, the mask, the greenish-colored fur, and the funny howl. "Hey, neat," seemed to be the consensus.

Boris was immediately relieved to find out that there were human children under the costumes, and he began to show off, making his mask move up and down over his muzzle, rolling over on his back to display the grotesque monster claws that his master had attached to his paws.

Parents who were chaperoning the trick or treaters came up to see what had so amused the kids on a night that was supposed to be filled with the screams and moans of little ghosts and goblins. They, too, laughed at Boris's outfit and congratulated Bob and Steffi on giving the kids something really special to talk about at their Halloween parties.

Bob managed a weak smile. Boris, his ultimate Halloween Horror, had been transformed from *trick* into *treat*. He glanced at his basset, surrounded by children in their costumes and masks, being hugged and petted and lapping it all up. *Hmmm,* Bob mused, Boris looked more like a horned frog than the Hound of the Baskervilles.

But, as Bob said to Steffi after the doorbell had stopped ringing and the trick or treaters had gone home to begin assessing their loot, there was also great art in making people laugh, as well as making them scream in terror.

Later, as he was washing off some of the green dye that had seeped into Boris's coat, Bob told Steffi that he thought next Halloween he would dress up Boris as a clown.

When the kids first heard the eerie, ghostly wailing emanating from the storm drains, they might have shuddered with the thought that the evil clown in Stephen King's horror novel *It* had materialized in High Point, North Carolina.

On March 14, 2002, a small crowd of residents gathered around a storm drain as city department workers Randy Clark, Jackie Hunt, and Kevin Vest lifted a manhole cover and tried to coax a six- to eight-week-old shepherd pup to come to them and be rescued. Obviously terrified after having been unceremoniously dumped to fend for itself by its owner, the puppy refused to budge. Later, Animal Control Officer Nelson Moxley said that on the day before he had gone in pursuit of the puppy after someone had reported two pups being dumped. He had managed to grab one of the discarded pups, a female, but he had lost the little male when it disappeared down a storm drain.

Now, Randy Clark, the supervisor, climbed down into the main pipe and attempted to grab the pup. Wrong move.

Randy ended up chasing the frightened puppy from one pipeline to another, running underground from street to street, playing what appeared to be a frustrating game of hide-and-go-seek. He recalled for the *High Point News-Record* that chasing a black-and-tan puppy through underground pipes with little light was not an easy task.

At last Randy saw the reflection of the puppy's eyes revealing the puppy's location as it tried to hide in the shadows. Randy said that as soon as he saw the pup's whereabouts, Randy moved so that he blocked the pup's escape. He didn't pick the pup up right away. He just petted him and touched his nose so that the pup would get used to him.

To the accompaniment of a chorus of cheers from the crowd gathered around the storm drain, Randy surfaced from the storm drain with the puppy in his hands, after an underground pursuit that had covered several blocks.

*O*n November 14, 2005, some hikers in the Great Smoky Mountains National Park heard a dog barking near their campsite off the Ace Gap Trail. They managed to track the sound to a deep hole about 300 yards away. The hikers very much wanted to help the dog get out of the dark, cavernous pit, but they estimated the hole to be about forty feet deep.

A construction worker at a nearby site thought that he might be able to rescue the unfortunate dog. He was able to get close enough to the edge of the hole to see a young, medium-sized dog known as a Mountain Cur, a breed that had been popular with pioneers in the region many generations ago, and a breed that remains a favorite choice for area residents. Try as he might, however, the builder wasn't able to reach the animal.

By the time park rangers arrived, it had grown dark, and they were unable to see or hear the dog. No one had any idea how long the poor thing had been down in the hole, so there was some concern that the dog, now silent, may have died. Rangers familiar with the location of the hole, believed the cavern to be far deeper than forty feet.

The next morning, Rick Brown and three other park rangers returned, determined to bring the young dog out of its imprisonment, regardless of the condition in which dog might be found. Cautiously, Rick climbed down into the hole, but he could find no trace of the dog.

After examining the terrain, he located another opening and a second drop off. Shining a light down into the second hole, he spotted the dog lying about another 30 feet below.

At first the dog lay still, but when Brown called to it, it struggled to its feet, looked up, and wagged its tail.

The team of park rangers rigged a harness and finally managed to lift the dog out about 3:00 P.M. that afternoon.

A tag around its neck identified the dog as Buck, and also gave the name and address of its owner.

When the park rangers contacted the man, he excitedly expressed his appreciation for Buck's rescue and his amazement that the dog was still alive. Buck had disappeared sixteen days before when the two of them had been out hunting raccoons. Somehow, the tough young canine had managed to survive more than two weeks trapped in the deep, underground prison.

The rangers told Buck's owner, that besides being half-starved and pretty well bruised and battered, the tough Mountain Cur was able to walk and seemed quite eager to go home.

When asked if the Great Smoky Mountains National Park planned to send Buck's owner a bill for the time and effort involved in the dog's rescue, a spokesperson for the staff said that such projects as saving a beloved dog's life fell under the category of being a good neighbor to the people who lived near the park.

*T*his past holiday season, Wendell Stevenson told us that he had recently read an article that advised parents against getting a puppy as a Christmas gift for their children. Among other points, the author of the article argued that the very atmosphere of Christmas morning with its chaotic cacophony of screaming children opening gifts, flashing lights, noisy visitors, ringing telephones, and parents bursting with good cheer might bring about permanent trauma and nerve damage to a newly weaned puppy.

The author also stated that receiving a puppy along with a whole Christmas tree full of gifts might equate the animal in the child's mind as being in the same category as just another toy—and in a few weeks or months, the puppy might be neglected along with all the other toys that had lost their initial appeal. And then, of course, there was the inescapable reality that a puppy was not a toy, but a living creature that required constant care, feeding, and companionship.

Wendell conceded that the author had some excellent points that every parent who was thinking of gifting a child with a Christmas puppy should consider, but he told us that when he was a child of eight back in the 1950s, he had received a special puppy directly from Santa Claus himself.

"I started working on my parents to get a puppy before Thanksgiving," Wendell recalled. "I said how nice it would be to have a puppy for a Christmas present. I was nearly nine, I reminded them, and my sister Pammy would be six in January. We were responsible children who understood that a little dog had to be fed, watered, and let out the backdoor to do its business in the yard, not the house."

But Wendell said his father would just smile and tell him, "Maybe next year when you're both older and *more* responsible."

There *had* been the incident of the turtle a couple of years back. Speedy had crawled out of its box and was found seven months later, dry as an autumn leaf, under the sofa. And then just the previous summer there *had* been the tragedy of the goldfish who suffered the fate of being overfed by two kids who could never seem to remember whose turn it was to shake the insect flakes in the bowl.

"I tried to point out that having a puppy was a lot different than having some old turtle with an American flag on its back and two goldfish who just swam around with their lips puckered," Wendell chuckled at the memory of his wheedling with his father. "But Dad would always counter with, 'Yeah, a pup is a whole lot more work and requires a world of care beyond shaking a few bugs into a bowl.'"

Wendell tried appealing to his mother, who countered with the classic parental ploy of referring his request back to his father.

Next, he tried the argument that his mother and father had had dogs when they were children.

"Yes," his mother could not deny the fact. "But we lived in the country on a farm. We had to have a dog to help with the livestock and to keep predators away at night."

His father had grown up in town. "But," he would state emphatically, "I didn't get my first pup until I was eleven, maybe twelve. A boy has a lot more sense and responsibility at that age."

The unspoken accusation was that at age eight Wendell had at least three or four more years to go before he had developed the requisite "sense and responsibility." And, Wendell had to accept the grim truth that his sister, being a girl and all, would probably take a whole lot longer.

Pamela Jane (Pammy) had a five-year-old's solution to the puppy problem whenever the two kids would discuss it. "We'll just ask Santa Claus to bring us a puppy!"

Wendell remembered that Pammy would utter this course of action with her blue eyes wide with pure innocence and with complete belief in the jolly, generous elf who lived at the North Pole.

"At five years old, Pammy still believed in Santa with all her heart," Wendell said. "I had those wonderful sugar-plum dreams dashed when I was six."

Wendell explained that his childhood images of benevolent elves in arctic workshops and mysterious bunnies who hid brightly colored eggs on Easter morning were irreparably altered on one fateful afternoon when he was six years old. It was about two weeks before Easter. Wendell was helping his mother carry in the groceries from the car when a sack that he was carrying jostled open.

Wendell couldn't help looking inside, but after he had done so, he said that there was a part of him that wished that he had never viewed the contents of that sack. His brain had bubbled and for a moment his vision blurred. He had to sit down on the sidewalk to catch his breath, letting the sacks of groceries that he was carrying spill out on the lawn. It seemed as though hours passed before he could speak, before he could find the words to frame his shock and disbelief. The sack that had sprung open contained the Easter Bunny's green grass and some Easter eggs. How could his mother possibly have the Easter Bunny's grass and eggs in a sack that she brought from a store, unless . . .?

Tears filled his questioning eyes, and when his mother saw that the sack containing the evidence of parental deception had accidentally opened and allowed Wendell to peek inside, she could only nod her head in silent affirmation.

"So *you* hide the Easter Bunny's eggs around the house?" Wendell asked. "You put them on the green paper grass by yourself? There really is no Easter Bunny."

Again came the silent confession of his mother's head, lowered now as whether she had been found out in some terrible crime of international consequences.

And then he had to ask the question that Wendell dreaded asking even more than if he might really have been an adopted child. "And Santa . . .?

"I remember how my heart pounded," Wendell said. "I prayed with all my being that she would laugh and say, 'Oh, well, Santa Claus is another matter altogether. Of course Santa is real.'"

But his mother only nodded again and finally spoke, asking a heartfelt request of him. "Please don't tell Pammy, Wendell. Let's allow her to believe as long as she can."

So just like that, Wendell told us, at age six, he was saddled with the unwelcome adult responsibility of deceit long before the course of normal events should have been allowed to play themselves out.

"I helped Pammy write her letter to Santa Claus, and she dutifully placed it in the box on which her kindergarten teacher had written in alternate red and green letters, '*To Santa: The North Pole,*'" Wendell said. "I figured at this point that all was lost. There was no Santa, and there was no Mom or Dad who would give us a puppy for Christmas."

On Christmas Eve, the Stevenson family went to the early church services and returned to eat their traditional meal of baked chicken, mashed potatoes, and corn. It was Pammy's turn to say grace on the family's regular rotational schedule, but on Christmas Eve, the family would hold hands and Dad said the prayer. As soon as there were a few seconds of silence after the group amen, Pammy added, "And please bring us a puppy for Christmas!"

After everyone had helped wash and dry the dinner dishes, the Stevensons gathered around the brightly lit and decorated tree in the living room and listened to Christmas music on the radio. When it was 9:30 P.M., it was time for the children to go to bed.

"I know Pammy went up the stairs with visions of coming down the stairs in the morning to find a puppy waiting for us," Wendell said. "I had no such expectations. I was resolved to another dogless year."

As he was drifting off to sleep, Wendell could hear the back door in the kitchen opening and closing as his parents carried in "Santa's" presents from the hiding place in the garage. He could also feel drafts of cold air moving up the stairs as they left the door open to make their back-and-forth trips in and out of the kitchen easier and quieter.

Sometime during the night, the miracle occurred.

At 7:30 P.M. sharp, Wendell and Pamela Jane came running down the stairs to see what Santa had brought them. As they started to tear into the packages, sending ribbons and bits of paper here and there, they were interrupted by the sounds of a dog whining.

Both of their mouths dropped open when they beheld the puppy cowering behind their father's easy chair.

"The black-and-white spaniel puppy looked as though he were starving," Wendell said. "His coat was matted and dirty. He was shivering in fear as he leaned against Dad's chair."

Pammy ran toward the pup, screaming her joy. "Santa brought us our puppy! Look, Wendell. It's our puppy!"

She started to kneel to pet the pup, then she straightened up quickly and wrinkled her nose. "Oh, my goodness, puppy. You stink!" she declared.

Their father and mother were coming down the stairs, shrugging into their robes as they came. Wendell could see by their expressions that the two of them were as surprised by the pup's presence as the kids were.

"What the . . .?" Wendell could hear his father's grumble of shock. "I thought we agreed that there would be no dog this Christmas?" his father said accusingly to his mother.

"Don't you dare look at me!" their mother answered with a return verbal volley. "I had nothing to do with this!"

"Santa Claus brought us our puppy," Pammy proudly announced. Then she added with a scowl, "But the elves forgot to wash him before Santa put him in the sleigh. He really smells awful."

When their mother got nearer the pup, Wendell could tell by the expression on her face that the family had gained another member. "Oh, George," she said in a sympathetic sigh. "Look at the poor thing. He's starved. And one of his paws is hurt. I'm going to get some of my chicken gravy to pour over some bread for the poor puppy to eat."

Wendell's father kept shaking his head and saying, "You have no collar, no dog tags. Where did you come from? Where in the world did you come from?"

"Every time Dad asked a question, it was as if he expected the puppy to have an explanation that he would accept," Wendell said. "And every time Dad would ask the same questions, Pammy was right there to give him her standard answer, 'Daddy, Santa brought him!'"

Once again, Pammy reached out her hand toward the pup, withdrew it, and announced, "Let's name him Stinky!"

"Mom and Dad laughed, and Mom said that since Santa brought him, we should name him after one of Santa's reindeer," Wendell said. "I saw how he was limping with his hurt paw in kind of jerking movement, so I said, 'How about Dancer or Prancer?'"

Unanimously, the family chose Prancer.

"And that's how we got our miracle puppy directly from Santa Claus," Wendell said. "Wisely, after we fed Prancer, Dad made us keep him in the mud room off the kitchen until after the veterinarian could give him his shots and a clean bill of health. Dad and Mom concluded that while they left the door open to carry in the gifts, the stray, homeless, hungry, and injured puppy had sought refuge in our home. Somehow, Prancer had managed to hide and not be seen by them as they placed the gifts around the tree. And he certainly gave everyone a big surprise when he was discovered on Christmas morning.

"Prancer matured into a wonderful family dog, who lived with us for over twelve years," Wendell said, concluding his account of his puppy miracle. "I was in college when I received the sad telephone call that he had left us. I chose to believe that Prancer hadn't really died, he had only gone back to the North Pole to help Santa answer the prayers of some other little boy and girl who wanted a puppy for Christmas."

*C*hristi, a one-year-old Labrador retriever pup, learned never to go on a goose chase, wild or otherwise, unless you have backup.

Christi was having a great time chasing the geese at the Somerset Beach campground near Jackson, Michigan. What an exhilarating feeling to charge at those feathered honkers and scatter them! What a wonderful sense of power to know that all these silly, long necked creatures feared her majesty. Even the gander, the obvious leader of the flock, was running from her. Emboldened, Christi zeroed in on the male, even following him into the lake.

Once Christi was a few feet off shore, the gander made its move. With a sudden strike of its powerful beak, the goose grabbed Christi by the neck and dunked her under the water.

Christi managed to fight herself loose of the gander and came up sputtering and very confused. This wasn't the way chase was supposed to be played. The gander was supposed to keep on squawking and running away from Christi's fierce barking and growling.

Amy Frederick, a lifeguard who was judging a sand castle competition, noticed the Labrador puppy in distress. She had been watching Christi's bold attack on the flock and knew that the pup had fallen into the gander's carefully staged trap. From past observations and her studies at Spring Arbor University, she knew that it was a common ploy of male geese to lead a predator away from the flock. Although Christi fit more into the category of a nuisance than a threat, the male goose was not in the mood to make a distinction. It had led the puppy into the lake on purpose and was now in the process of purposefully drowning her.

Amy Frederick later told Michigan's *Jackson Citizen Patriot* that there was a large group of campers present that afternoon and there were at least forty children participating in the sand castle contest. Suddenly all eyes were on the desperate struggle occurring in the lake. The gander had managed to maneuver the pup to the middle of the lake and was continuing to dive at Christi with its large beak and hold her under the water.

Amy said she could clearly see that the pup was becoming exhausted and that it would soon be drowned. "I couldn't bear to let a puppy drown," she said, "especially in front of all those kids."

The lifeguard dove into the water, approaching the scene of the drowning with the same seriousness and determination that she would invest in saving a human life. When she reached Christi, the pup was so tired that she immediately reached out for Amy and laid her paws on her shoulders.

Fellow lifeguard Tiffany Rowe came to help in a pontoon boat and positioned the craft between Christi and the murderously angry gander. The two women hoisted the trembling puppy up on the pontoon and brought her safely to shore.

David Luke, the campground's executive director, said that the kids "just went crazy with their cheering and clapping" when Amy and Tiffany delivered Christi to the beach.

Christi learned a valuable lesson in the ways of the animal kingdom: Just because a prey appears to run away in fear doesn't mean it doesn't have a bigger plan to kick your rear.

*I*n late January 2004, a motorist called the sanitation department in Duluth, Georgia, to report the body of a dead dog lying in the road. Later that same day, the sanitation department workers picked up the mangled body of a young beagle pup that had obviously been struck by a car. The little corpse was placed in a bag and sent to the Washington-Wilkes Humane Animal Shelter for incineration.

A few minutes before cremation, conscientious shelter director Gloria Wheatley opened the bag to see if the puppy had any license or identification tags or if it matched the description of any missing dog. She just might be able to save some family some grief and give them closure over the death of a beloved pet if there were any clues to the pup's identity.

Gloria had just opened the bag when, as she said later, she immediately shut the bag. She didn't believe what she was seeing. The puppy was still alive. In fourteen years of handling and cremating dead animals, it was the first time such a thing had has ever happened to Gloria.

She took the puppy to a veterinarian, who found it cold and unresponsive. The doctor said that the beagle pup had been thrown into a coma after the accident, and had awakened just moments before it would have been incinerated. Even though the puppy had appeared to rally, the doctor gave him little chance of surviving through the night.

Veterinary technician Becki Walker was touched by the valiant puppy's determination to live, and she volunteered to provide care for it. Recalling the Bible story about Jesus raising Lazarus from the tomb after he had been declared dead, Becki named the beagle pup "Lazarus."

Throughout the next day, Becki monitored Lazarus's condition, and, from time to time, she would hold him. After two days of such tender care, Lazarus remained in a coma, but his brain was showing signs of activity. Encouraged and determined, Becki put nutrients in a syringe and fed it to the pup.

Lazarus's back legs, which had been paralyzed, began to move. Amazingly, after three days, he was on his feet, but exhibiting problems with his motor skills due to the severe brain injury he sustained when the car struck him. Becki maintained her monitoring of Lazarus's progress, admiring the beagle puppy's will to live and his determination to keep going every day.

Linda Blauch, president of the Companion Animal Rescue League in Duluth, agreed to accept Lazarus as a foster dog after he was ready to be released from the hospital. When he first arrived at Linda's home, Lazarus would walk around in circles to the right. He yawned a lot, as if unable to pull enough air into his lung. His tongue would sometimes stick out, and he moved with a dazed look in his eyes.

Towards the beginning of his stay, Lazarus was not responsive to Linda Blauch or the other dogs in the household. Gradually, Linda noted that he began to behave more like a normal puppy. The first time she heard Lazarus bark was during dinner. Beagles, she commented, are famous for their desire to eat.

Lazarus soon became known as the miracle puppy. He had been struck by an automobile, left for dead, was nearly incinerated, lapsed into a coma, and now, after the careful and attention of a number of dog-loving humans, he had returned from the dead—just as his namesake had.

*B*abycake, a bull terrier, was barely eight months old and a new member of the Easley household in Chattanooga when she had a chance to become a hero. Mike Easley was asleep in his upstairs bedroom after a hard drive from Tucson for the trucking firm that he had been working for since March 10, 1999, when his mother Colleen suffered a heart attack in her bedroom in the basement.

Immediately sensing something terribly wrong, Babycake ran upstairs to Mike's bedroom. Urgently, she began barking and banging her tough little head against the door.

Mike mumbled a couple of "go aways" and "get losts" and one or two less civil words, before he gave in, got out of bed, and opened the door to let her into his room. Thinking she just wanted to play, Mike bent over to pick up a yellow ball and threw it out of his room into the hall. "Go fetch . . . and leave me alone. *Please,* leave me alone, Babycake," Mike grumbled.

Babycake whined when she saw her owner get back in bed, and she pulled away the blankets and started yanking on Mike's arm.

Suddenly realizing that the puppy was trying to tell him something, Mike got up and followed Babycake downstairs where he found his mother lying unconscious next to her bed. Mike dialed 9-1-1, and the paramedics arrived within minutes.

Colleen spent two days in critical condition, but she fully recovered, thanks to a very smart—and very alert—puppy.

*S*yndicated columnist Terri Schlichenmeyer recently told us this story about the innate intelligence of puppies. Her husband Jim had accepted a very good position with a worldwide company that required him to be gone for months at a time.

As a result of these disruptions in what had become a normal schedule, Terri said they had had some episodes of canine "acting out." In Terri's words:

"Last Monday, we had one of *those* days when Truman and Lucy did almost everything in their power to annoy me. Jim's been gone for a little over two months, and we have still these days now and then.

"Anyhow, Monday night, after we had all made our peace with one another, I was laying in bed, talking to my fur kids. I said, 'Maybe what we need to do is have play breaks, huh? Maybe you just need my undivided attention now and then. Why don't you guys bring a toy upstairs once in awhile, to remind me about this, okay?' This is somewhat contradictory, as we've taught them to leave their toys downstairs. Nothing in the world is worse than stepping on a soggy, furry, squeaky toy in the dark at 3:00 A.M. I talked to them for a little longer, shut off the light and went to sleep.

"Tuesday afternoon, I was working away in my upstairs office, when I notice it had suddenly become very quiet. Very *suspiciously* quiet. I had heard the dogs trump up the stairs, so I looked down. On the floor on my right, Truman was sleeping with a toy in his front paws. On my left, Lucy was asleep next to her toy."

*L*ike any obedient children, they had done just as Mommy had asked. We are certain that anyone who has shared his or her life with a puppy can relate instances similar to Terri's experience of the time the pups appeared to understand every word that was spoken to them.

Who do you think is smarter—your canine puppy or a wolf puppy? Consider your choice carefully. Is the wolf, hailed by Native American tribes as the great teacher, the more intelligent? The wolf must live in the wilderness against incredible odds and survive by its wits and cunning.

Or, is your jolly roly-poly puppy, living large by your side, warm and well-fed in your home, the more intelligent of the two cousins?

In Budapest, Hungary, at Eotvos Lorand University's Department of Ethology, research fellow Adam Miklosi has been studying the cognitive abilities of man's best friend since 1997. The experiments have revealed that dogs have far greater mental capabilities than scientists had previously thought. The cumulative evidence demonstrates that dogs' intelligence manifests in their relationships with people and that dogs may make better cognitive study subjects than primates.

Until recent tests and studies, perhaps the majority of scientists believed that the process of domestication over the centuries had dulled dogs' intelligence. Studies conducted in the early 1980s revealed that wolves, from which dogs probably descended, could unlock a gate after watching a human do it once, while dogs remained apparently baffled by the process, even after observing the actions several times.

The conclusions drawn from the "unlocking the gate" tests were never accepted well by Vilmos Csanyi, the retired head of Adam Miklosi's department. Vilmos, a dog owner himself, suspected the dogs used in the tests were awaiting their owner's permission to open the gate. Well-trained dogs, always eager to please and keep harmony at all costs, would regard the opening of a gate as a violation of their master's rules.

In 1997, Vilmos and his colleagues at tested twenty-eight dogs of various ages, breeds, and degrees of bonding to their owners, to see whether the domesticated pooches could learn to obtain cuts of meat on the other side of a fence by pulling on the handles of dishes while their owners were present. Dogs who enjoyed a close bond with their owners did not do as well in this test as outdoor, ownerless dogs. But when the dogs' owners were permitted to give their obedient canine companions verbal permission to fetch the meat, the gap between the groups of dogs vanished.

Dogs excel at imitating people. "We thought it would be very difficult for dogs to imitate humans," Vilmos said to journalist Colin Woodard, writing for *The Christian Science Monitor* ("Why Your Dog is Smarter Than a Wolf," October 26, 2005). "Chimps have great difficulty doing so, even with their larger brains. But it turns out [dogs] love to do it. This is not a little thing, because they must pay attention to the person's actions, remember them, and then apply them to their own body."

Vilmos and his colleagues demonstrate in countless experiments that even young puppies have got "smarts." According to Vilmos, "Dogs' unusual ability and motivation to observe, imitate, and communicate with people appears to be with them from birth."

Dogs are "very motivated to cooperate with and behave like people," says Vilmos. "That's why dogs can do things no other animal can do."

"If there are no dogs in Heaven, then when I die I want to go where they went."
—*Will Rogers*

"If I have any beliefs about immortality, it is that certain dogs I have known will go to heaven—and very, very few persons."
—*James Thurber*

When Merlin Hess was twelve, he was struck by a pickup truck while riding his bicycle down a country road on the way home from school. In and out of consciousness throughout the ambulance trip to the hospital and while they were preparing him for surgery, Merlin thought he was dying and he believed that he had heard a doctor say that even if he lived, he would never walk again. While he was unconscious under anesthesia and for most of the next two days, Merlin felt that he journeyed to heaven and spent time with the angels and the spirit of his puppy that had been accidentally shot by a hunter.

Today, more than forty years later, Merlin can still vividly recall the memories of a time that seemed to be spent in a beautiful apple orchard in heaven.

"I could take deep breaths and smell the lushness of the place," Merlin said. "And it felt so good to run! If my legs were gone on Earth, at least I was able to run in the afterlife. And then I started to laugh and run around the orchard."

Merlin believed that it was his laughter that brought the angels to investigate the disturbance in the tranquil orchard. "These two beautiful, glowing angels were suddenly just standing there right in front of me, and they wanted to know why I was laughing, so I told them that I might never walk again on Earth, so I better run as fast as I could in heaven."

Then, Merlin said, it was as if he was somehow being passed back and forth between two worlds. "I would close my eyes in the hospital room and open them in this void of terrible darkness. Or I would close my eyes to keep back the awful blackness, and I would open them back in the hospital room."

Merlin began to become very frightened. It seemed to him that he was dying. In the depth of his despair, he was transported back to the lovely orchard where the two angels awaited him.

"This time when I returned to the angels, they had my puppy Bojangles with them," Merlin said. "A pheasant hunter had shot Bojangles in our farm field alongside the road a couple years before. The hunter claimed he thought Bojangles was a pheasant, and he didn't even get out of the car to check it out before he pulled the trigger. I really missed that pup."

Merlin calmed down and felt less fearful when he saw his puppy with the angels, but he was smart enough even at his age to realize that the angels were doing their best to make him comfortable and at ease in heaven.

"Back in the hospital room, my parents heard me call out Bojangles's name, and they, too, thought for certain that the spirit of the dog had come to take their son home to heaven," Merlin said.

Then, Merlin recalled, the strangest thing happened. Bojangles appeared to come bounding into the hospital room, just as full of life and spunk as when he was a pup on the farm.

"I thought that I was dying then for certain," Merlin said, and he cried out, "Dear, Lord, if I am dying, please let me have a good run with Bojangles right now.

"And just like that I seemed to get up out of my crushed body, and my soul self started to run after Bojangles. He ran down a hospital corridor and we went right through a wall. I followed him, and it was as if I passed through some kind of doorway to paradise. The sun was bright and shining, and Bojangles was just ahead of me in this beautiful green meadow. There were clover blossoms, butterflies, and all kinds of wildflowers. I remember seeing a little brook running across the meadow, and I saw the angels beckoning to me."

While he sat petting Bojangles, Merlin was shown a panorama of his life experiences in the smooth surface of the water. He saw the surgeons operating on his shattered legs once again, and he felt that they were fixing them so he would be able to walk.

He remembered the angels smiling at him and telling him that he would be returning to his body so that he could be healed and grow up to become a minister or a teacher. "I chose teaching," Merlin said. "I knew that I couldn't be a conventional pastor and preach that dogs don't go to heaven, because I saw Bojangles there, very much a dweller in paradise."

*W*hen she was ten years old, Kendra R. was badly burned when she accidentally fell into a campfire while on an outdoor weekend in the Catskills with her parents.

"I remember the pain being excruciating," Kendra recalled. "First, there was the seemingly endless ride to the nearest hospital with my semi-hysterical mother at the wheel of our van. Dad had burned his hands pulling me out of the campfire and beating out the flames that were burning my clothes and my flesh. I was in and out of my body during that long drive. It hurt too much to stay in for too long, so I elected pretty much to stay above it all in my spirit body."

Kendra told us that she underwent a lot of the same progressions of consciousness and awareness that she has heard so many people who survived near-death-experiences describe. "I became aware of a long, dimly lit tunnel, and my spirit self began to enter it. Even as I went into the opening, I could hear my mother's voice sounding as if she were very far away. She was telling me to stay awake, not to die, not to leave them. All her words sounded like she was speaking from an echo chamber."

About the time that her mother was parking the car near the entrance to a hospital's emergency room, Kendra felt her consciousness moving deeper into the tunnel, into a space of almost total darkness.

"I saw a light, a brilliant light at the end of the tunnel," she said, "and I began moving steadily toward it. Just as I was about to reach out and touch it, it disappeared and was immediately replaced by what looked to me like some kind of zoo. There were animals everywhere. And then I thought that I must have stopped in animal heaven.

"I walked up to beautiful collie dogs and little poodles, and they seemed pleased when I stopped to pet them. There were horses and cattle and pigs, and I even saw some monkeys. There were lots of birds, like parrots and parakeets and canaries."

Then Kendra had the thought that if this was really animal heaven, then she should be able to see Akumba, her beloved Pomeranian, who had passed away just a few months before. She had had the dog since she was three and she missed Akumba so much, because she had *really* loved him.

"I heard a familiar bark, and I turned to see Akumba," Kendra said. "But he didn't look like he did when he got sick and older. He looked just like he did when he was a little puppy—and he was glowing as if he were a doggie angel. Beautiful, multicolored rays emanated from Akumba's body."

Kendra reached out to touch her beloved puppy, but Akumba suddenly turned and ran away from her.

"I thought, *Oh, no. Please don't play your silly keep-away game up here in heaven,*" Kendra said. "I was becoming kind of frightened and lonely and wondering if I was dead, and if I was soon to be going on to people heaven. I really needed to hug Akumba and get some of his love."

Akumba led her into some kind of maze that had been constructed of interwoven bowers of brightly colored flowers.

"That's when I realized that he was not running away from me. Akumba was leading me somewhere." Kendra recalled.

After a time Kendra and Akumba stood before what appeared to be a small cave in the side of a mountain.

"When I looked into the cave, I could see doctors and nurses working over my body, treating me for the awful burns. I knew that Akumba seemed to be telling me that

I must return to all that pain on Earth. He rubbed up against my hand and reached out his tongue to lick my fingers. I remember crying out, 'Oh, I love you, Akumba,' and then almost as soon as his little pink tongue touched my fingers, I felt myself falling into the cave and shooting back inside my physical body."

The next day while Kendra's doctor was on her rounds at the hospital, she asked Kendra who Akumba was.

Both Kendra and her mother, who was sitting at her bedside, laughed at the sound of Akumba's name.

Dr. Sanchez smiled, but her forehead wrinkled in puzzlement, not in on the joke. "When you were regaining consciousness after emergency treatment for your burns," she told Kendra and her mother, "you were telling someone named Akumba that you loved him."

Kendra recalled how Dr. Sanchez just shrugged and walked away laughing when she told her that she had been brought back from heaven by Akumba, her puppy angel.

*O*ur late friend Bryce Bond was one of the world's most respected explorers of the unknown, a published author, and the host of *Dimensions in Parapsychology,* a popular television program for many years in the New York metropolitan area. Besides sharing an interest in investigating the unexplained, Bryce shared our love of dogs. Before he made his own transition to the "other side," he received astounding proof that our dogs also go past the grave.

One of Bryce's dearest friends and companions was his French poodle, Pepe, a dog small in size, but large in love. Both Bryce and his wife loved Pepe very much, and he became the child that they had never had. They shared with him a happy balance of love, and Pepe returned that energy of tenderness and affection to them.

Although Pepe had been a puppy full of zest and vigor, he developed cancer when he was older. As the cancer became increasingly painful for Pepe, the Bonds sought professional help for him. But all the veterinarians said the same thing. Pepe was too far gone. Nothing could be done but to put him to sleep.

"I took Pepe's head in my hands and held him very close to me," Bryce said. "I was half-crying, half-telling him that it was all right. I was with him. He licked my fingers. I kissed him on the top of his head and whispered from my heart, I love you. Goodbye, my friend.'"

The doctor administered the lethal injection, and Pepe relaxed and fell asleep. There were no twitching muscles or any other signs of pain. Pepe had peacefully gone home.

Bryce and his wife placed their dear Pepe's body in a wooden box, and began the seven-hour drive to her home in Virginia. "We had agreed to bury Pepe there on my wife's family's peanut farm. He had loved it there, because he could run free without any big-city restrictions."

The next day, the Bonds covered Pepe with his favorite blanket and placed some of his favorite toys with him in the wooden box. Then they closed the lid for the last time, nailed it shut, buried the box, and covered the area with pine branches.

"The loss of anyone or anything connected to you by the bond of love is painful," Bryce said. "But I knew that as long as I had memory, I would always be connected to Pepe. He was the child I never had—and he was also a teacher to me."

Three years after Pepe's death, Bryce was lying in bed ready for sleep. "My physical body was just about to drift into the sleep state when I felt something jump up on the bed and land at my feet. At first I thought it was part of my dream cycle, but the something began to circle around, then settle on my feet with physical weight and body heat. My eyes were closed, so I kept them closed. I wanted to *experience* the experience!"

In Bryce Bond's consciousness, he knew that it was Pepe come to pay a visit, for the dog had always joined him in bed in just such a manner. *Thank you, God!* he rejoiced in his heart.

Pepe then got up and slowly walked the length of Bryce's body until he reached his head. Bryce was able to feel a smallish body depressing the mattress with actual physical weight as it moved upward.

"Then Pepe brushed against my face about seven times," he said. "I kept my eyes tightly shut. I was overjoyed. I wanted this to happen. I feared that if I opened my eyes this wonderful experience would cease."

Bryce reached out in the darkness, his eyes still closed.

"I felt his tail with one hand, his cool, wet nose with the other," he said. "Next I moved my hand to his stomach, and I felt him breathe. His stomach was soft and warm to the touch. I could smell the scent of him without any mistake. It was my Pepe!

"In spite of my joy, I did not open my eyes throughout the entire experience—which lasted for about ten minutes. Then, at last, Pepe was gone. I once again gave thanks to God for the experience."

After the visitation, Bryce remembered that he fell in a deep and very peaceful sleep. When he awakened the next morning and replayed the events of the previous evening in his mind, he noticed that there were clumps of black hair wedged under each of his fingernails—*poodle hair.*

"I trembled with excitement over the additional proof that Pepe had given me to bring peace to my heart and to demonstrate that he was all right," Bryce said. "Later, I had the hairs analyzed by a veterinarian and a forensic chemist. It was, indeed, poodle hair. And as any poodle owner knows, poodles don't shed. Pepe had provided me with physical proof that consciousness survives. Such events are gifts from God!"

*O*ur friend Sandra J. Lund has often said that it always bothers her to hear someone say that animals don't have spirits. Sandra, an author, included inspirational messages devoted to spiritual energies within the animal kingdom in her book, *The Kyrian Letters: Transformative Messages for Higher Vision.* Sandra and her husband Denton, a well-known artist specializing in Western themes, live today in Wyoming, but Sandra has often reflected upon an earlier time when she spent marvelous years with Sheila, a German shepherd puppy, who grew to mean so much to her.

In the early autumn of 1975, Sandra's young daughter was riding her bicycle in their neighborhood in Huntsville,

Alabama. Sandra had gone to visit her next-door neighbor, and when she returned home, she found her family sitting in the living room waiting for her. Lying on the floor was a large German shepherd dog, whose paw was bleeding all over the gold carpet.

The next day, Sandra drove the beautiful dog to a veterinarian to have her wounded paw treated. Later, at the grocery store, she purchased cans of dog food and some bones.

"She was such a loving dog that I grew attached to her very quickly and really wanted to keep her," Sandra said. "We decided we couldn't do that until we had made an effort to find her owner. So, we placed an ad in the local paper, providing all the necessary information."

The same day that Sandra's "found" ad appeared in the paper, the German shepherd owner's "lost" ad was printed directly beneath it in the same column.

That evening Sandra received a call, and the dog's owner, a young man in his twenties, came to their home to see if the dog was indeed his.

"I hoped she wasn't his," Sandra admitted, "but deep down, I knew. The minute he walked through the door to our home, the German shepherd made it very clear that she belonged to him. Her name was Buffy, and she was so very overjoyed to see him."

The young man kept telling Sandra how much he appreciated her taking such good care of Buffy. He insisted upon paying the veterinarian bill, but Sandra wouldn't let him.

As she packed up the cans of dog food, Sandra told the young man how much she had enjoyed having Buffy around and how much she would miss her.

He understood. "I plan on breeding Buffy," he said. "And if she ever has puppies, I'll give you one because of the care that you gave her."

Sandra was fully aware of the transience of promises made in a passionate moment and then forgotten with the passage of time. As the weeks passed, the family went on with their lives, and Sandra's few days with Buffy slipped deeper into her memories.

Then one day late in the spring of 1976, there was a knock at their front door. Sandra opened it, and there stood Buffy's owner.

"Do you remember that German shepherd dog that you helped last year?" he asked her. "Well, she had puppies, and I have one for you."

Sandra went with him to his car, and there in a little box was the cutest German shepherd puppy that she had ever seen. "She was only eight weeks old, but she had ears which stood straight up, that seemed far too big for her tiny body."

Sandra explained that sometimes German shepherd puppies must have their ears taped so they are able to remain straight. Such would not be the case with this dog.

"The puppy was light tan with dark markings, and was blessed with the most beautiful brown eyes," Sandra said. "She immediately stole my heart, and I always thought of her as a reward for a good deed—as a precious gift from Buffy and her young owner."

Sandra named the puppy Sheila, and she remembered that puppyhood was not easy for the little German shepherd because she possessed a very mischievous nature.

"She forced everyone in the neighborhood to retrieve their Sunday papers early in the morning or else the papers would end up shredded on my lawn—much to my embarrassment," Sandra said. "She was so joyous, however; and when she would look at me with her big, brown eyes, I couldn't stay angry very long."

As Sheila grew up and became a mature lady, Sandra said, she remained loving, gentle, and loyal. "She never ceased to be one of the most treasured gifts in my life," Sandra said.

Sheila loved to run, and when the family moved to Colorado, she delighted in camping in the mountains with them.

It was around Christmas in 1982 that Sandra noticed that Sheila was limping. The problem didn't go away, so Sandra took Sheila to the vet about a month later. His diagnosis indicated that she needed surgery on a ligament in one of her back legs. Sandra decided to have it done, regardless of the cost, because Sheila loved to run so much.

The surgery appeared to be successful, and Sheila seemed to be healing well. However, one evening as Sandra was rubbing Sheila's neck, she felt the dog's glands were swollen.

Sandra took Sheila back to the veterinarian, and he placed the dog on antibiotics. They did no good. Sadly, cancer had soon spread throughout Sheila's entire system.

"As I looked at this beautiful and beloved friend, I knew that although she never made a sound, she was suffering," Sandra said. "I knew that her quality of life would never be the same again. Making the decision to put Sheila to sleep was the most painful and difficult thing that I had ever done."

Sandra said that she wept a great deal before taking Sheila to the veterinarian, and she shared with us a beautiful piece that she wrote dedicated to the memory of her beloved companion. Entitled "One Moment In Time," the words may help all those who may find themselves in similar, very saddened circumstances:

"I wish a sense of peace could shower upon me and cleanse me from the agony I feel. A beautiful lady is dying to this life. A selfish part of me wants her to stay, wants just a little more time. But, then, in the area of loving, is there ever enough time?

"In this moment, I wonder if I will ever find the quality of the relationship we have. Will I ever allow myself to be bonded in love to the same degree?

"Somehow, the loss of Sheila's physical form does not seem so great when I remember the quality of the relationship. I find myself having been blessed with seven years of her presence. It is because of the nature of this love, this all-accepting love, that makes me yearn for more time. When life is really good, we don't want change, for we can envision nothing better.

"Yet, she must go from this world, and I must release the warmth of her form—although I know that I shall never release the memories. And I must go on in the struggles of this world, thankful that our lives came together, and together we journeyed for a time.

"The highest tribute I can pay Sheila is to learn what she has taught me and to allow my heart to open once again to another all-accepting love.

"What made our friendship so special is that it was the closest that I have been to the exchange of unconditional love. We were two life forms journeying in time, in acceptance, and in love for each other's essences. And what in life is better than this?"

*I*t is not within the purpose or scope of this book to answer the great question of whether dogs have souls or whether people will meet their dearly departed puppies in Heaven or the afterlife. But if, as the wise and holy teachers admonish us, "To err is human and to forgive is divine," then it would often appear as though our dogs have moved a step or two ahead of us on the path of spiritual evolution. There is no greater demonstration of unconditional love than that which one finds in the devotion of a puppy.

It has always seemed to us that one of the greatest gifts that the Creator has given humankind is the opportunity to establish a communications link with dogs, a species separate and unique from ourselves, but so devoted to our well-being. We don't need to wait for a spaceship to land with an extraterrestrial crew to be able to attempt verbal or telepathic communication with another species. We have a marvelous, loving terrestrial species that has been standing by our side for the last 140,000 years, just waiting to *bond* with us, to *blend* with us, and to *become one* with us.

We have always respected dogs as sovereign entities, allied with us, yet different from us. If it is true that we learn our virtues from the friends who love us, then we would like to think that throughout our life journey our canine companions have taught us something of loyalty, devotion, integrity, patience, and love.

For us, the planet would be a very bleak place if it were not for puppies. Indeed, the good Lord may have given us dogs to bless us, to make our present lives on Earth more bearable, and to prepare us for the unconditional love that we are certain to find with the angels in heaven. If the loving Divine Creator indeed runs the universe, then our puppies will be there to greet us when we leave this life.

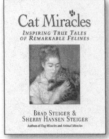